Breaking Free of the
CO-DEPENDENCY
TRAP

Breaking Free of the
CO-DEPENDENCY
TRAP

BARRY K. WEINHOLD, Ph.D.

JANAE B. WEINHOLD, Ph.D.

STILLPOINT PUBLISHING

Products and technologies for creating the EXTRAordinary life.

For a free catalog or ordering information, write:
Stillpoint Publishing, Box 640, Walpole, NH 03608
or call: 1-800-847-4014 TOLL FREE
(Continental US, except NH)

This book is manufactured in the United States of America.

Text design by Irving Perkins Associates, Brattleboro, VT

Cover design by Bellwether Peers, Peterborough, NH

Typesetting by NK Graphics, Keene, NH

Published by Stillpoint Publishing, a division of
Stillpoint International, Inc.
Box 640, Meetinghouse Road, Walpole, NH 03608.

Published simultaneously in Canada by
Fitzhenry & Whiteside Ltd., Toronto

Library of Congress Card Catalog Number 88-062957

Weinhold, Barry K. and Janae B.

Breaking Free of the Co-dependency Trap

ISBN 0-913299-49-9

19 18 17 16 15 14 13 12

We dedicate this book to all the individuals, couples and partners who are serving as pioneers in creating new forms of relationships.

Contents

Foreword

Breaking Free of the Co-dependency Trap is a welcome addition to the emerging literature on co-dependency. The Weinholds are expert clinicians. Their offering is crucial for establishing the legitimacy of co-dependency as a true life-threatening clinical entity.

Using their knowledge of developmental psychology, Barry and Janae see co-dependency as the failure to complete one or more of the important developmental tasks of early childhood. They see the problem as especially focused on a failure to complete the early task of separation—sometimes called second birth or psychological birth. This fits well with my own definition of co-dependency as a dis-ease of lost selfhood.

The Weinholds' developmental approach differs radically from the medical approach which sees co-dependency as permanent, progressive and incurable. Developmental stuckness can be remedied. There is hope and promise for all of us.

The greatest sense of hope in this book results from the precise and practical tools for recovery with which the Weinholds present us. These are proven methods used by the authors both to help their clients and to work on their own co-dependency issues. Janae and Barry "walk the walk" as they "talk the talk." This is crucial. I demand it of my treatment people at the Life Plus Co-dependency treatment unit.

I believe with the authors that the most crucial issue in

recovery is the creation of a new relationship committed to working out the interdependent intimacy. The core of co-dependency is the shame-based ruptured self. This self-rupture resulted from a broken relationship (Chapter Eight). Therefore it takes a new relationship committed to this work to heal it.

This book is far too rich to highlight in a foreword. I am amazed at the thoroughness of this treatment. Part One is a true summary of the state of our knowledge about co-dependency. Part Two covers all the major tools for recovery. My heartfelt advice is for you to read and study this book carefully and then read it again. BRAVO!!! Barry and Janae!!! This book is a gift!!!

John Bradshaw
National Director
Life Plus Co-dependency
Treatment Unit
Los Angeles, CA
January, 1989

Acknowledgments

We would like to acknowledge the ground-breaking work that Alcoholics Anonymous has provided in the treatment of addictions and, more recently, the important work of Co-Dependents Anonymous which is based on the AA model. These grass roots organizations are reaching millions of people who otherwise would not have the necessary support to deal with their addictions.

We also would like to acknowledge the pioneering work of John Bradshaw, who hosted the widely acclaimed PBS series "Bradshaw On: The Family." This series broadened significantly the understanding of millions of people about dysfunctional family structures and how they contribute to the causes of addictive behavior.

Finally, we wish to acknowledge the ground-breaking work of Riane Eisler, author of *The Chalice and the Blade* and co-director of the Center for Partnership Studies in Pacific Grove, California. Dr. Eisler's framework helped us better understand the societal roots of the problems of co-dependency. In addition, we greatly appreciate her support for this book and her editorial assistance with the final manuscript. We feel like partners with her in helping to create a partnership society.

At a more personal level, we would like to acknowledge our parents, Kern and Betty Weinhold and Leland and Milly Branyan, our four children (Gregory, Margie, Mark and Chad), our clients, members of CICRCL and our colleagues who helped us in various ways to formulate our ideas for this book. We have tested most of the material on ourselves, our clients and our students and know that it works. Our experience with all these people has taught us what we needed to learn in order to write this book.

At the production level, we would like to thank our editor, Caroline Myss, for her helpful suggestions, editing and personal support. We also would like to thank the following people who assisted in the production of the manuscript: Paul Burke for his copy editing and Kris Fisher and Elaine Elsner for their typing.

Introduction

This book examines the basic causes of co-dependency, which occurs in about 98% of the adult population and is responsible for most human misery. Co-dependency is learned dysfunctional behavior and is the result of the failure to complete one or more of the important developmental tasks during early childhood.

Causes of Adult Co-dependency

From birth to two or three years of age, the child completes a series of developmental tasks, but the most important psychological task is the development of basic trust between mother and child. If this basic trust or bonding is completed successfully, it allows the child to feel safe enough to explore his or her world and eventually, about age two or three, to complete the so-called second birth or psychological birth. The psychological birth occurs when the child learns to become psychologically separate from his or her mother. Among other things, with the successful completion of this task, the child is able to function on internal power, so to speak, rather than having to rely on others to direct his or her life. The child develops a sense of self that enables him or her to learn to accept responsibility for his or her actions; to learn to share, cooperate and handle aggression; to respond appropriately to the authority of others; and to verbalize feelings and learn to deal effectively with fear and anxiety. If the task is not completed successfully, the child becomes psychologically dependent on others for these things and has no strong sense of self, separate from others.

Co-dependency in adults exists when two psychologically dependent people form a relationship with each other. In such a relationship, each person supplies a part of what it takes to create a psychologically complete or independent person. Since neither is able to feel and act very independently of the other person, the two people *tend* to stick together like glue. As a result, the focus of each person is on the other person, not on himself or herself. The relationship *cannot* grow because it is always left up to the other person to make it happen. This leads people to try to control each other and to blame their problems on each other, and to expect others to always behave the way they want them to behave. In this way people also avoid focusing on their own inner awareness and self-development. The focus is always outward, not inward.

In this book we present a radically different framework for understanding the causes of co-dependency than the ones currently in vogue. We call our approach a "developmental approach" as opposed to the popular medical approach that regards co-dependency as a primary illness. A primary illness is defined as one that is permanent, pervasive, progressive and terminal. We believe co-dependency is a learned disorder that results from arrested development or a developmental "stuckness" that can be remedied. In the recovery process, persons who have co-dependent symptoms need to:

1. understand the developmental causes of their disease

2. remove the obstacles that resulted in their developmental stuckness

3. become more fully aware of themselves and the ways they respond to situations so they can feel more free and make better choices

4. exercise effective control over their own lives

5. develop higher and higher levels of human effectiveness.

The Medical Model: No Recovery

The prevailing medical model states that co-dependency is either a genetically inherited illness, with unknown causes, or a disease associated with alcoholism and dysfunctional families. In either case it is considered *incurable*. According to the medical model prognosis, the best you can hope for is long-term treatment and a support system that will help you avoid the addictive agent (other dependent people) and, therefore, keep you from forming destructive co-dependent relationships. Support groups and psychotherapy are seen as essential to help you stay on the non-addictive path because, without this support, you would likely choose an addictive path. Your fate is seen as outside your conscious control and the result of internal and subconscious addictive reactions that can easily overpower your conscious mind. In other words, you cannot hope to be free from the disease.

A New Definition of Freedom

Our approach to co-dependency actually starts with a new definition of freedom. Whether our behavior is the result of free will or is the result of conditioned responses with little or no exercise of free will is an issue that has been discussed for centuries. Neither extreme in its absolute form has been proven to exist in reality. What is really important is whether or not you *feel* free. Do you feel relatively free to control your own life or do you feel that others control your life to a large extent?

The two prevailing definitions of freedom have been:

1. freedom from some kind of bondage.

2. freedom from freedom itself, seeing freedom as an illusion that doesn't exist.

The medical approach seems to be founded on a deterministic view that says it is impossible to exercise free will over co-dependency.

A third definition of freedom supports the developmental approach and involves self-awareness. *We believe true freedom comes from within and not from without.* True freedom cannot be achieved by focusing on the social 'evils' outside yourself. To be free you must also focus on the psychological evils that exist inside you. By becoming more aware of your inner self and the reasons why you react the way you do in certain situations, you can begin to develop a sense of mastery over the forces that seem to control you and keep you from feeling free. The more you become aware of all your internal psychological parts and can orchestrate or direct them consciously, the more freedom you will experience in your life.

Two Traditional Types of Recovery Programs

There are two traditional approaches to recovery from co-dependency. In the first type of program, we include most of the so-called 12-step programs such as AA (Alcoholics Anonymous), OA (Overeaters Anonymous) and CoDA (Co-Dependents Anonymous). This type of recovery program promises full recovery for those who successfully "work their program," but it tends to place too much emphasis on the disease model. Members of 12-step groups are told that they are sick and powerless over substances, activities or people. While this helps ease some of the guilt about the pain they may have inflicted on their family or friends, it can sometimes prevent them from looking at the psychological issues involved in their addictions. Because of this emphasis on external causes, a "Higher Power" is frequently viewed as an external force that controls and rewards sobriety. Bill Wilson, the founder of AA, intended for the "Higher Power" to facilitate a deep spiritual awakening that he believed was necessary for full recovery. For all its limitations, this is a very important first step to recovery. This type of recovery program has helped millions of people move away from these devastating problems. If people do not stay away from those things over which they have lost control, they cannot benefit from more extensive recovery programs.

In the second type of recovery program [advocated by Ernie Larsen (1985), Robert Subby (1984) and Sondra Smalley (Schaef 1986)], the focus shifts to helping people rebuild their lives and learn how to have more effective relationships. However, there is still a belief that the disease of co-dependency can only be arrested, not cured entirely. These programs suggest, however, that some of the problems of co-dependency in relationships can be cured. Some people involved in this type of recovery program have begun to see that co-dependency may not be a primary illness, and they have put more emphasis on seeing it as the result of ". . . self-defeating learned behaviors, that are greatly exaggerated and complicated by a pathological relationship to a chemically dependent (or co-dependent) person . . ." (Larsen 1985:17).

New Recovery Approach

The developmental approach discussed in this book is a third kind of recovery program. It goes much farther than the other two approaches. It is founded on the belief that co-dependency is not a primary illness but a learned developmental disorder that can be overcome with the proper information, tools and support. *It focuses on full recovery and the fullest development of human potential that is possible.* It provides more hope and a more positive attitude regarding recovery.

We believe in this approach because we have been successful in using it on ourselves as well as our clients. We have seen people fully recover from the devastating effects of co-dependency. The process was not an "easy" one for us or for our clients to use, and it is not necessarily quick. It took us a number of years and lots of work to get where we are today. By using the tools presented in this book, however, you will begin to see an improvement in your relationships right away.

As more and more people are successful in breaking out of the co-dependency trap, it will become easier and quicker for everyone else. Part of the reason it has been so difficult for many people to change is that many of our society's cultural beliefs and practices have supported the maintenance of co-dependency. As people change, so will these cultural attitudes and beliefs. We will no longer accept a highly limited view of human behavior.

Another unique feature of this book is that it focuses primarily on the tools for recovery rather than merely describing the problem of co-dependency and the methods of recovery. We believe that the most powerful form of recovery may come not from therapy, but from committed relationships. If you have a relationship in which both people are committed to seeing the relationship itself as a tool for healing, then individual or couples therapy, support groups or working on yourself alone can serve as support to the therapeutic process that is occurring in the relationship.

Peter Russell, in his book *The Global Brain* (1983), predicts that the Consciousness Age will follow the Information Age. He sees the Consciousness Age developing before the year 2000. "This would represent a time when the needs for food, material goods and information were adequately satisfied and the major thrust of human activity would be able to move on to exploring our inner frontiers. Self-development would become our prime goal . . ." (p. 185).

We agree with Russell and believe that this book is based on that view, which will give more and more people the vision of who they really are and provide them with tools to realize their fullest possible development.

Part One

CO-DEPENDENCY REVISITED

CHAPTER ONE

Co-dependency: Getting Stuck in Infancy

AN OVERVIEW OF THE PROBLEM

We believe that approximately 98% of all Americans suffer from some of the major effects of what is now called co-dependency. Estimates indicate that less than 1% of these people are fully aware of the effects of co-dependency and even fewer of them are taking steps to correct these effects.

Some of the major symptoms of co-dependency are:

- feeling "addicted" to people

- feeling trapped in abusive, controlling relationships

- having low self-esteem

- needing constant approval and support from others in order to feel good about yourself

- feeling powerless to change destructive relationships

- needing alcohol, food, work, sex or some other outside stimulation to distract you from your feelings

- having undefined psychological boundaries

- feeling like a martyr

- being a people-pleaser

- being unable to experience true intimacy and love.

To make matters worse (if that is possible), co-dependency is usually treated by the medical community (including most therapists) as a primary illness. If you are diagnosed as having "caught" co-dependency (like one catches a cold), your doctor or therapist is likely to consider your illness to be permanent, pervasive, progressive and perhaps even terminal.

According to most doctors, therapists and writers, you will *never* recover from it. The best you can hope for is that you will be able to "hang around" with other recovering co-dependents. If you attend support meetings regularly and work on yourself, you will not get worse *and* you might not be as bad as you used to be before you started treatment.

This sounds very depressing, doesn't it? Well, this book should not depress you. It can help you lift your heavy burden. It presents a positive new approach to the treatment and healing of co-dependency that is based on over thirty years of research and experience in successfully treating co-dependency.

Assumptions of the New Approach

This approach is based on the following assumptions about the causes and treatment of co-dependency:

- *It is not a primary illness.* It is a disorder caused by the failure to complete important developmental tasks in early childhood. The major task, often referred to as the psychological birth, should have been completed by about age two or three. However, in 98% of the population, it doesn't get completed on schedule. Since parents usually haven't completed this task for themselves, they can't help their children and may even subconsciously resist the attempts of their children to complete this important task.

- *It is a cultural phenomenon.* Because of the pervasive nature of the problem, our whole culture can be called co-dependent. When one looks at the problem from a cultural perspective, it becomes obvious that major institutions in our society support co-dependent behavior. The social structure we have created may actually be dependent upon this behavior continuing. Throughout modern history, most societies have been structured so that some groups are ranked above others, such as men over women and management over labor. With one group more powerful and in control of the resources, co-dependent relationships can be easily created and maintained. If people begin to change their co-dependent patterns, it will bring changes to the larger social structure.

- *Co-dependent patterns continue to recycle.* If this developmental task is not completed on schedule, it is carried along as excess baggage that interferes with the completion of other developmental tasks during childhood. If it is not completed during later childhood or adolescence, it is then carried on into adulthood where it continues to disrupt people's lives. The natural learning style of humans is to repeat what we are trying to learn over and over until we finally learn it. This is why co-dependent patterns repeat.

- *It is a healing in progress.* Co-dependency, with all its dysfunctional symptoms, is, in reality, a healing in progress. There is a natural drive in all of us toward healing and completion. We simply need to cooperate in that healing process to make it work.

- *Tools and understanding are necessary for recovery.* When people understand the basic causes of co-dependency and are given the tools and support they need, they can and will heal themselves and eliminate the negative effects of co-dependency from their lives.

- *It requires a systemic treatment approach.* Because all parts of our social system support co-dependency, it is necessary to use a "systemic" approach as well as an individual approach to treating co-dependency. Therapy with couples, families and in groups seems to be an effective way to help individuals break co-dependency.

- *There is no blame.* It takes two or more people to create co-dependency. Therefore, one person cannot be blamed for having created a co-dependent relationship.

A NEW DEFINITION OF CO-DEPENDENCY

Based on the above assumptions, co-dependency is defined as a psychological disorder caused by a failure to complete one of the most important developmental tasks of early childhood, that of establishing psychological autonomy. Psychological autonomy is necessary for the development of the self, separate from parents. Margaret Mahler and her associates (1968) did extensive research to help us understand the course of development that helps the human infant move successfully from psychological oneness at birth to psychological autonomy at about age two or three.

She found that people who have successfully completed this developmental task are no longer dependent upon people or things outside themselves to guide their way. They have a solid inner sense of their uniqueness and of who they are. They can get close to others without fearing a loss of self. They can effectively meet their needs by asking others directly when they need help. And finally, they can maintain a positive self-image even when they receive criticism from others. Mahler also discovered that a failure to complete this vital task can rob people of their full humanness and force them to live severely limited lives dominated by fear, compulsive behaviors and addictions.

The successful completion of the process of developing psychological autonomy, according to Mahler, requires two conscious parents who have dealt with enough of their own psychological hang-ups to be able to help the child. In order to assist the child in successful completion of the second birth, parents need to:

- bond solidly with the child

- accept the child as he or she is, not as the parents would like him or her to be

- allow for the full expression of feelings and accept and understand the feelings and needs of their child

- support and encourage the child in the healthy exploration of his or her world by using at least twice as many "yeses" as "nos"

- effectively "kid proof" the immediate environment in order to allow the child to safely explore his or her world

- encourage the expression of independent thoughts, feelings and actions appropriate for the child's age

- be available to provide understanding, support and nurturing when the child needs it

- model effective psychological independence by asking directly for what they want, expressing their own feelings effectively, setting appropriate limits and negotiating directly to get their needs met, rather than using power plays and games. Research suggests that young children learn appropriate behaviors by watching the behaviors of others around them.

Characteristics of Co-dependency

When you look closely at the main characteristics of a co-dependent person, you begin to see an unmistakable pattern of behavior that is more characteristic of an infant than of a fully functioning adult. Below is a list of the common characteristics of co-dependency. As you read the list, place a check mark next to those items you recognize in yourself. Also, notice how many of the characteristics you associate with children around the age of two or three.

If you are co-dependent you tend to:

- be unable to distinguish your own thoughts and feelings from those of others (you think for and feel responsible for other people)
- seek the approval and attention of others in order to feel good
- feel anxious or guilty when others "have a problem"
- do things to please others even when you don't want to
- not know what you want or need
- rely on others to define your wants or needs
- believe that others know what is best for you better than you do
- throw temper tantrums or collapse when things don't work out the way you expect them to
- focus all your energy on other people and on their happiness
- try to prove to others that you are good enough to be loved
- not believe you can take care of yourself
- believe that everyone else is trustworthy. You idealize others and are disappointed when others don't live up to your expectations.
- whine or pout to get what you want
- feel unappreciated and unseen by others
- blame yourself when things go wrong
- think you are not good enough
- fear rejection by others
- live your life as if you are a victim of circumstances
- feel afraid of making mistakes

- wish others would like or love you more
- try not to make demands on others
- be afraid to express your true feelings for fear that people will reject you
- let others hurt you without trying to protect yourself
- not trust yourself and your own decisions
- find it hard to be alone with yourself
- pretend that bad things aren't happening to you, even when they are
- keep busy so you don't have to think about things
- not need anything from anyone
- experience people and life as black and white—either all good or all bad
- lie to protect and cover up for people you love
- feel very scared, hurt and angry but try not to let it show
- find it difficult to be close to others
- find it difficult to have fun and to be spontaneous
- feel anxious most of the time and don't know why
- feel compelled to work, eat, drink or have sex even when you don't seem to get much enjoyment from the activity
- worry that other people will leave you
- feel trapped in relationships
- feel you have to coerce, manipulate, beg or bribe others to get what you want
- cry to get what you want
- feel controlled by the feelings of others
- be afraid of your own anger
- feel helpless and powerless to change yourself or your situation

- feel like someone else needs to change in order for you to feel better.

Someone once said that you will know you are co-dependent if you are dying and someone else's life flashes in front of you. The characteristics of co-dependency reflect an outer focus to life—the need to look to others to direct your life in some important area. Co-dependency in a relationship occurs when two people, each seeking from the other what they feel they don't have, come together to form one complete person. Each feels that he or she cannot function well without the help of the other person. This prevents personal growth and development. Eventually one of the two grows tired of the unholy alliance and tries to change things. Lacking information on the causes of co-dependency or the tools and support necessary to break the pattern, he or she normally will fail and fall back into a co-dependent relationship once again.

Recovery From Co-dependency

The self-directed method of recovery from co-dependency is seen as an expanded 12-step process and is briefly described as follows:

1. Admit that there is a problem that you cannot solve with your current information and resources.

2. Learn the real causes of your problem.

3. Learn to identify the symptoms of the problem as they exist in your current relationships.

4. Stop blaming your problems on others.

5. Stop blaming and criticizing yourself for your mistakes and a lack of perfection.

6. Stop using power plays and manipulations to get what you want.

7. Be *willing* to ask for what you want all of the time.

8. Learn to fully feel and express all of your feelings.

9. Take steps to develop a strong inner awareness of your thoughts, feelings, values, needs, wants and desires.

10. Learn to define your psychological boundaries in relation to others.

11. Learn to be close to others in order to get the necessary information, nurturing, mirroring and bonding to help heal yourself.

12. Learn to live in a fluid state of relationship with your true self and with others, allowing for the development of your fullest potential.

The recovery process usually takes time and effort for most people. We generally recommend that people plan to spend about one month in recovery for every year that they have lived. Thus, a thirty-six-year-old person can expect to take three years of working on recovery before completion can be achieved. However, you can and will see significant progress toward this completion almost immediately. Couples in a committed relationship can also accelerate the process, especially if they use all of the available recovery resources. The authors advocate that you consider using as many of the following recovery resources as possible.

Resources for Recovery

- A committed relationship with another person who is also willing to break his or her co-dependency patterns

- Couples therapy or family therapy with a therapist who uses a "systemic" approach to treat co-dependency

- Support groups where other people are working on similar issues. Some Co-Dependents Anonymous (CoDA) and Adult Children of Alcoholics (ACOA) groups might provide you with this support.

- Selected reading of books and articles on recovery from co-dependency

- Courses and workshops that provide information on the causes and treatment of co-dependency

- Tools to help you explore your inner realms, such as meditation, breath work, journal keeping, yoga, dream analysis, art work, mirror work, inner child work, feeling work, and some of the martial arts such as Tai Chi and Aikido. These will be explained in detail in Part II of the book: The Stages of Recovery.

Case Example of Co-dependency

I (Barry) received a call from Mary, a former student, who seemed quite worried about her thirty-one-year-old daughter, Sara, who had been very depressed and suicidal. Mary asked me if I would have time to see Sara as soon as possible. I found a space in my schedule and Mary said, "I'll call her and see if she will come to see you and then call you back and let you know." That was my first clue that co-dependency might be behind this problem. I said, "Mary, I would prefer that Sara call me directly to set up the appointment, if that is all right with you." There was a brief silence on the phone as Mary pondered my request. Finally, as if she hadn't thought of that option, she said, "Well, I guess that is okay. I'll tell her to call you."

In my first session with Sara, after taking a brief history, I asked her to rate her depression on a scale of 1 to 10, with 10 being the most depressed she could imagine. Sara replied, "About nine." I asked her about her relationships and about what it was like growing up in her family. Her answers confirmed my initial suspicion that she was hooked into co-dependent relationships. Her parents had overprotected and controlled her as a child. Her mother was highly critical of her, always demanding perfection. Her father was distant and her parents fought constantly.

She had very low self-esteem and had trouble with people invading her psychological space. She had trouble saying "no" to co-workers and bosses who often asked her to do extra work. In her relationships with men, she always tried to please her partner but never felt successful and often felt unloved. She tended to see people as all good or all bad and was frequently disappointed in people. She had tried to live an independent life, hoping to convince herself and others that she didn't need to be close to anyone. The truth was that she was desperately lonely and had built a thick wall around herself. Now the wall was starting to crack and she didn't know what to do.

She seemed shocked when I asked her if she thought her mother and father might come to therapy with her. She thought she could get her mother there but not her father, who didn't believe in therapy ("that's for crazy people"). I explained that I believed that she had never become psychologically autonomous from her mother and that she would probably continue to have unsatisfying relationships until she broke the bonds that were keeping her from using her own internal power.

As homework, I asked her to make two lists of the unfinished business she still had with her mother. On the first list I asked her to write down all the things that she remembered her mother saying and doing to her when she was a child that she now sees as harmful to her as an adult. On the second list I asked her to write down all the things that she wished her mother had said or done to her when she was a child that she now thinks, had she gotten them, would have made her life easier.

Her mother came with her to the next session and Sara began with her lists. I explained that the first list represented all the things for which she hadn't completely forgiven her mother. She probably still had resentment about these things. The second list, I explained, contained those things she was still looking to her mother or mother substitutes to provide for her instead of getting them for herself. She decided to start with the first list, and I explained that she first needed to express the resentment directly to her mother before she could forgive her.

Sara started with, "You were always criticizing me and I could never do anything right for you. I felt awful." Mary replied, "Yes, I did criticize you and that was my own need for perfection that I put on you. I know I shouldn't have done that.

I was so ill-prepared to be a parent and felt overwhelmed most of the time." The pattern was much the same with the other items on Sara's list. Mary would acknowledge the truth in Sara's complaint and also express her guilt at not doing better. When the session ended, I felt that the process was not complete, so I asked Mary if she would return with her daughter next week. She agreed.

At the beginning of the next session, I found out that neither one liked what had happened at last week's session and that they almost didn't come back. Sara said, "I feel badly telling my mother these things. All she does is feel more guilty." Mary said, "I had trouble sleeping several nights this week. I was really upset." I decided to focus on Mary's guilt.

I asked her what it would take for her to forgive herself for not doing a better job of raising her daughter. She said she didn't know.

Then I said, "Could you ask your daughter to forgive you?" Mary looked scared, like she wanted to leave. Finally she said, "Yes, I think I might be able to do that sometime." Obviously she wanted to put it off. I said, "Your daughter is sitting right here, and this is an excellent opportunity for you to get this resolved." After some more thought she turned to her daughter and said, "Sara, will you forgive me for what I did to you when you were a child?" Sara replied immediately, "Of course I forgive you, Mother." Mary flinched as if to discount what Sara had said. When I saw Mary do this, I asked Mary to go inside and feel the forgiveness in her body. She closed her eyes and said she felt a black shaft going down to the pit of her stomach. Suddenly it was filled with light and her stomach stopped hurting.

Then I asked Mary to look inside and see if she needed any more forgiveness. She said she felt a sick place even deeper inside of her that needed to be healed, so she asked again, "Sara, will you forgive me?" This time Sara reached over and hugged her mother and again said, "Yes, Mother, I forgive you." The two embraced and cried. After they separated, I asked Mary to look inside again to see if that had gotten down to that sick place deep inside of her. Again she closed her eyes and, as she sat there, two buttons of her dress, which was buttoned down the front, popped open. Sara, seeing this, exclaimed, "Mother, the guilt is popping out of you." We all laughed and then they embraced again.

Suddenly I understood the dynamic that had created their co-dependent relationship. I said, "Mary, you have been relating to Sara with your guilt and not with your love, and Sara feels that discomfort. She may believe that you really don't want to do things with her and that the only reason you are doing things with her is because you feel guilty or feel sorry for her. This probably contributes to her low self-esteem. She doesn't want to ask you for anything, fearing that you will say 'yes' from your guilt. She needs to know that you really want to be with her and want to do things with her and that you will say 'no' if you don't want to be with her." Sara confirmed my statement and added, "I want a relationship as an equal friend with you, not with you as my guilty mother. I, too, feel guilty sometimes when I ask you to do things with me, but I don't tell you. Will you agree to a new relationship with me based on love and not on guilt?" Mary said, "Yes, I want that very much."

As the session came to a close, I said to Sara, "Do you want to continue in therapy to work further on your depression and low self-esteem?" Sara looked straight at me and said, "No, I don't think I want any more therapy at this time. I want to work on this by myself for a while. I feel stronger and more confident that I can take care of myself better now. This work with Mom has really helped me. I have lots of questions to ask her about things that happened when I was a child, and I think she can give the answers I need." Then she added, "When I'm ready to deal with my dad, I'll probably be back and drag him along. I think I can convince him to come with me."

This case illustrates how *quickly* major life-long co-dependencies can be broken. Obviously, it is not always possible to get parents and/or children together to resolve these issues, and it isn't necessary. If Sara's mother had not cooperated and come to therapy with her, I would have played the part of Mary. I believe we would have achieved similar results. What is necessary is to get a clear picture of the co-dependent patterns and then discover what holds the co-dependency together. Guilt or shame are common emotions that keep co-dependent relationships going.

AWARENESS ACTIVITY: HOW CO-DEPENDENT ARE YOU?

The following self-inventory may help you determine the degree to which co-dependency is present in your life. Please answer these questions honestly. Usually the first answer that comes to you is the most honest and most accurate.

A Self-Inventory
Typical Characteristics Of Co-dependent People

Directions: Place a number from 1 to 4 in the space before each question to indicate the degree of your response.

    1 = Never
    2 = Occasionally
    3 = Frequently
    4 = Almost always

( ) I tend to assume responsibility for others' feelings and/or behavior.
( ) I have difficulty in identifying my feelings—happy, angry, scared, sad or excited.
( ) I have difficulty expressing my feelings.
( ) I tend to fear or worry how others may respond to my feelings or behavior.
( ) I minimize problems and deny or alter truth about the feelings or behavior of others.
( ) I have difficulty in forming or maintaining close relationships.
( ) I am afraid of rejection.
( ) I am a perfectionist and judge myself harshly.
( ) I have difficulty making decisions.
( ) I tend to be reactive to others rather than to act on my own.

( ) I tend to put other people's wants and needs first.
( ) I tend to value the opinion of others more than my own.
( ) My feelings of worth come from outside myself, through the
opinions of other people or from activities that seem to validate
my worth.
( ) I find it difficult to be vulnerable and to ask for help.
( ) I deal with issues of control by attempting to always be in control
or, the opposite, by being careful never to be in a position of
responsibility.
( ) I am extremely loyal to others, even when that loyalty is unjus-
tified.
( ) I tend to view situations with "all or none" thinking.
( ) I have a high tolerance for inconsistency and mixed messages.
( ) I have emotional crises and chaos in my life.
( ) I tend to find relationships in which I feel "needed" and attempt
to keep it that way.

Scoring: Add the numbers to get a total score. Use the following
ranges to help interpret your level of co-dependency:

    60-80 – A very high degree of co-dependent patterns
    40-59 – A high degree of co-dependent patterns
    30-39 – Some degree of co-dependent and/or counter-
                dependent patterns
    20-29 – A few co-dependent and/or a high degree of counter-
                dependent patterns

CHAPTER TWO

The Medical Model: Stuck in Hopelessness

AN OVERVIEW OF TRADITIONAL APPROACHES

Co-dependency has been defined by an overwhelming majority of the medical and therapeutic community as a primary disease that has an onset, a definable course and a predictable outcome. It is considered by most to be incurable. People who are diagnosed as co-dependent are told they can only hope to advance to a "recovering" stage but will never be fully "recovered." This attitude permeates the addictions field primarily because the study of co-dependency, which was once called "co-alcoholism," has its roots in the study of alcoholism. Alcoholism is currently seen by the American Medical Association as a primary disease from which there is no chance of full recovery.

Alcoholics Anonymous, which began in the late 1930s, developed a set of key assumptions about alcoholism that initially promised full recovery as an attainable outcome. Originally the various forms of medical treatment of alcoholism were intended to serve as an adjunct to the AA grass-roots approach. However, over the past ten years, those forms of treatment that consider alcoholics as victims of an incurable disease have taken over as the dominant forms of treatment not only for alcoholism, but now for eating disorders, compulsive gambling and co-dependency as well. Stanton Peele, in his new book, *How the Addiction Industry Captured Our Soul* (1989), states that we can't help people recover from an addiction by convincing them that their cause is hopeless and then teaching them to define themselves forever by their addictions. He says, ". . . we tell people they can never get better from their 'diseases' and then . . . we actively recruit new addicts, finding them at the drop of a hat or declaring that they are alcoholics on the basis of their first drunken episode." This medical approach to the treatment of addictions, which is increasing in popularity, is being aggressively promoted by medical lobbyists and commercial private practitioners into a multi-billion dollar a year business. (Figarette 1988)

KEY ASSUMPTIONS OF THE MEDICAL MODEL

- Addictions are genetically inherited.
- Once you have the addiction you will always have it.
- You will probably marry someone who will help you maintain your addiction. The only hope to move toward recovery is to trust something or someone outside of yourself—a higher power, a 12-step program or group, a sponsor or a therapist.
- Addictions are diseases that can lead toward death.
- Alcoholic family systems, often with multiple patterns of addictions, are the source of co-dependency.
- Behavioral patterns learned in an alcoholic or a dysfunctional family can be changed or modified only with great difficulty.
- You will ALWAYS be considered a victim of your addiction.

Traditional Definitions of Co-dependency

Based on these assumptions, most approaches to co-dependency define the problem in rather limited ways. First, co-dependency is usually defined as a primary illness, linking it with alcoholism and drug addiction. As a result, much of the literature focuses on the negative aspects of co-dependency, reinforcing the deep sense of shame that one might feel as a result of being identified as having a co-dependency illness. In the addictions field, there is a belief that by calling alcoholism or an eating disorder (and now co-dependency) an illness, it reduces the shame of seeking help. While it is true that calling alcoholism and other addictions 'diseases' has eliminated some of the social stigma connected with seeking help, it has introduced another form of addiction: the belief that you can never recover from the illness. Shame may prevent you from seeking treatment until the situation reaches a crisis point. By this time, you may have reached a deep state of hopelessness and despair that has to be overcome before the real problem can be addressed. By calling co-dependency an illness, the stigma of seeking help or admitting you have a problem may be made less traumatic. However, you may find yourself trapped in another co-dependent system that supports hopelessness. Even cancer patients receive more hope than this.

The emphasis on addiction as a primary disease is supported by the medical profession for good reason: economics. By classifying addictions, such as alcoholism, eating disorders and co-dependency, as diseases, insurance companies are asked to pay for treatment. If the figures on the pervasive nature of co-dependency are correct, this creates a tremendous windfall opportunity for physicians and therapists who receive insurance payments. Initially, at least, it would be a windfall. If all the so-called co-dependents in this country began seeking insurance-reimbursed treatment for co-dependency, it could become a nightmare. It might ultimately contribute to the collapse of the health insurance industry. If that were to happen, the collapse of the medical industry (which is largely supported by the insurance industry) might soon follow. It is critically important to look at the long-term effects of this emphasis on the disease model and to look for a better approach to the treatment of co-dependency.

A Case Example

Elaine's struggle with anorexia, an eating disorder, illustrates this point. As a child she experienced several traumatic shocks: being in an automobile accident that demolished the family car, coming home to discover that the house had burned down during a family outing and witnessing violent disputes between her parents that eventually ended in a bitter divorce. Elaine tried harder and harder to be the perfect daughter, hoping that somehow, through her own "perfection," she could prevent such catastrophes.

By the end of her junior year in high school, she was so thin that her mother feared for her health. She sought treatment for Elaine with several therapists who focused on working with Elaine's symptoms. After several months of no success with therapy and a decrease in Elaine's weight, her mother finally sought help from a physician. The physician immediately persuaded her mother that hospitalization was necessary. The hospital in a large city several hundred miles away had just recently created a live-in clinic that kept patients for several months while putting them through an expensive, insurance-subsidized program of recovery. The program emphasized the medical aspects of the disease with extensive medical and psychological tests and the use of prescription drugs. The clinic, built especially for the treatment of eating disorders, was designed to simulate a comfortable, homelike environment. The cost of treatment averaged $445 per day, with six weeks being the average length of stay, making the total cost of treatment $18,690.

Elaine's mother, convinced by the physician's authoritarian manner and Elaine's previous lack of success in therapy, consented to a six-week period of hospitalization. This necessitated Elaine's withdrawal from high school classes in her senior year and separated her from her family. Her mother was required to make long drives to visit her during the treatment and was expected to pay large sums for the charges that their insurance did not cover.

As a result of this treatment, Elaine became more compliant to her doctor's and her mother's wishes by eating more regularly. She continued to take medication and have continuing therapy to help her maintain her still severely limited functioning. In the long run, Elaine's fate is uncertain because only the *symptoms* were treated. One could assume that she remained a co-dependent, recovering anorexic and continued to live a limited life at home where her mother and her doctors could monitor her health and her life.

Another Approach

Instead of seeing Elaine as "the identified patient" in the family and treating her individual symptoms, it would have been more useful to treat the whole family. By looking at the pattern of relationships and working directly with the whole family to discover its disturbances, the core cause of her anorexia might have been revealed. By employing a family systems therapist to explore the family traumas of which Elaine was a part, it might have been possible for Elaine to express her stored-up feelings about her childhood traumas. Furthermore, it could have provided Elaine with the support she needed to complete her psychological birth so that she didn't need to use rebellious, dysfunctional behaviors as a way of separating from her family.

This family system approach might have been used on an outpatient basis with a therapist who had access to contingent medical support if it became useful or necessary. This would have permitted Elaine to remain at home and complete her psychological work with the people who had helped create the problem. As it was, only Elaine was treated, making reentry into the family system difficult. This approach also served as a replay of the loss and abandonment issues of her childhood and offered little or no hope of full recovery.

Because of the systemic nature of most addictions, people who try to change themselves are often met with massive resistance from parents, spouses and children. One recovering alcoholic had to experience numerous drunk-driving accidents—the last one resulting in his hospitalization for six months—and the loss of his wife and children in a divorce before he finally admitted that he had a drinking problem. Hearing his admission, his wife said, "Oh, dear, you don't have a drinking problem; you've just got to control your anger." Even his parents and friends resisted his admission of alcoholism and tried to talk him out of it. (Andrews 1987) People who are stuck in co-dependent relationships don't want anything to change. They are afraid that any change will mean they will be forced to take care of themselves. That is a risk that most co-dependents do not want to take.

RECOGNIZING CO-DEPENDENT AND HEALTHY MESSAGES

Co-dependent Messages	*Healthy Messages*
You're stubborn.	You can ask for what you need.
You should be perfect.	You can make mistakes.
Hurry up.	You can take your time.
Overadapt to others.	You can think about what you want.
Try hard.	You can do it.
You need to be strong.	You can feel and have needs.
You're special.	You can be yourself.
Work hard.	You can play and have fun.
You're confused.	You can think and feel at the same time.
You're stupid.	You can think and be effective.
Don't be so selfish.	You can be spontaneous.
You're dull.	You can be creative.
You're sick or crazy.	You can stay well.
Always be right.	You can admit you are wrong.
You need to distrust others.	You can trust others.
Be careful.	You can relax and let go.
You need to be dependent to be loved.	You can be independent and be loved.

The Stages of Recovery

This book recognizes three stages of recovery. The first one focuses on breaking the primary addiction to the substance or process. In this approach you can be a "dry drunk"—that is, sober, but still not dealing with your underlying psychological issues or family patterns. Your dysfunctional relationships probably continue, but your primary addiction such as alcohol may be replaced with another addiction such as work or food. This approach uses participation in AA or other similar support group networks as its major treatment modality.

The second stage of recovery involves rebuilding your life and relationships that were damaged during the period of addiction. During this stage you learn more about the traumas of your childhood and replace dysfunctional attitudes and behaviors with more functional ways of living and thinking. While the goal of this stage is healing your wounds, it still recognizes addictions, such as co-dependency, as primary illnesses from which you can never fully recover.

This book is about a third stage of recovery, one in which addictions are recognized as the result of an incomplete task of development in childhood. This approach focuses on helping people to complete the necessary developmental tasks and reach full recovery. It also uses a systemic approach and avoids labeling the co-dependent person as sick. It is full of hopefulness and offers one the possibility of reaching his or her full potential as a human being. This is a radically different approach from the disease-oriented model that has been sold to the American public. This developmental model looks at the scientific research about human development and concludes that human beings are wonderfully self-correcting creatures. If people are given correct information and skills, they can complete any of the important developmental tasks of childhood that they failed to complete on schedule, and thus rid themselves of co-dependent behaviors.

Summary

Disease-focused kinds of treatment, which offer little or no hope of full recovery and do not take a systemic view, are typical of the approaches used by the bulk of the medical profession. Rather than searching for the roots of addiction in the family system or by examining the culture, the medical profession frequently zeroes in on the most obvious symptoms, trying to eliminate them with drugs and their traditional tools. If we continue to focus on finding a "cure" for addiction (as if it is an "illness"), whether it be substance abuse, such as alcoholism, or a process abuse, such as workaholism, we will fail to find the real causes of addiction. This approach cannot work, especially with such a pervasive problem as co-dependency. It is time to look at co-dependency in a broader context, one that does not judge individuals but recognizes co-dependency also as a cultural phenomenon that grows out of the evolution of our species. We, as a species, are richly endowed, and we are on the threshold of finding effective ways to support the exploration of our human potential. By breaking our co-dependent patterns as individuals and by creating ways to initiate social change that will support these changes, we may be part of the greatest personal and social transformation in all of recorded history.

CHAPTER THREE

The Co-dependent Culture

DOMINATOR VS. PARTNERSHIP MODELS

Most people in the addictions field are looking at co-dependency as an individual or family problem. Some are beginning to examine it as a "systems" problem. A few people are beginning to look at it as a problem of our whole society. Ann Wilson Schaef, in *Women's Reality* (1981) and *When Society Becomes an Addict* (1987), identifies two systems that she sees are in conflict: the White Male or Addictive System and the Emerging Female or Living Process System. While Schaef's categories and perspectives have been useful in pointing out some obvious differences in ways of thinking, they still do not reach into the depths of the co-dependency syndrome.

It is the work of Riane Eisler in *The Chalice and the Blade* (1987) that provides a more in-depth historical review of culture on our planet and gives an evolutionary look at two basic forms of relationship which she calls the dominator and partnership models. She provides a detailed analysis of the challenges and problems that each has created. Eisler's study includes the whole of human history (including prehistory) and the whole of humanity (both its male and female halves). She weaves together evidence from art, archeology, religion, social science, history and numerous other fields to help create a new story about our cultural origins. Her perspective helps transcend the "battle of the sexes" for control and domination in which many contemporary feminists have been involved. Eisler's view is much longer and deeper.

The Partnership Society

When Eisler delved into prehistory, she found numerous legends and archeological records that described an earlier form of civilization in which the culture was organized quite differently from what we know today. According to these records, there were large areas in Europe and the near East which enjoyed a long period of peace and prosperity. The social, technological and cultural development of the existent society followed a steady move upward. This civilization, which she identifies as a *partnership* society, was based on unity, cooperation and mutual need. The society valued the life-giving and nurturing qualities that we might consider to be "feminine." Burial tombs of this era reveal a wealth of statues and artifacts devoted to the worship of a female Diety, The Great Mother. These artifacts, along with their ancient art, myth and historical writings, indicate a deep reverence for life, caring, compassion and nonviolence.

The archeological evidence also reveals that this early social structure was based on equality. Power, risk-taking and rewards were shared without regard to gender. This cooperative approach helped create unity and harmonious relationships among people and between the people and the planet. Eisler contends that at a point in prehistory, perhaps about 3500 B.C., this 30-40,000 year era began to wane, and the qualities of the feminine were gradually replaced with more masculine values that structured a completely different kind of civilization that she identifies as a *dominator* society.

The Dominator Society

Dominator societies, according to Eisler, exalt the qualities that we stereotypically associate with masculinity and value life-taking and destructive activities, such as conquest and warfare. This social structure, which is based on inequality, generally ranks one part of society over the other. Even though the cultural values are what we today think of as 'hard' or more 'masculine,' dominator societies can be either matriarchal or patriarchal. The higher ranked group holds the power, takes the risks and reaps the rewards, leaving the lower ranked group to powerlessness and, often, poverty. Rather than linking people cooperatively, they rank people competitively, creating a hierarchy that is ultimately supported by force or the threat of force. This creates an atmosphere of distrust and separation.

In studying Eisler's model of social structures, it becomes clear that the dominator model creates a co-dependent society, and the partnership model creates an interdependent society in which people work cooperatively to support each other. Extending her model in this way, a comparison of the two might look like this.

The Co-dependent Society	*The Interdependent Society*
– creates hierarchies that are ultimately backed by force or the threat of force	– creates heterarchies in which people are linked together by common need
– the higher ranked group in the hierarchy holds the power of decision making while the lower ranked group is powerless	– the heterarchical group shares equally in decision making

The Co-dependent Society	*The Interdependent Society*
– the higher ranked group assumes responsibility, risk-taking, the means of production and reaps the rewards, while the lower ranked group provides the support and labor and reaps minimal rewards	– the heterarchical group shares equally in the risk-taking, responsibility, capital investment, means of production, rewards, labor and support
– uses comparative 'you or me' thinking	– uses cooperative 'you and me' thinking
– a co-dependent form of relationship between the two holds the system together	– an interdependent form of relationship within one large group holds the system together
– values life-taking and destructive activities such as war and exploitation	– values life-generating and nurturing qualities such as compassion and nonviolence
– utilizes rigid sex roles	– utilizes fluid sex roles
– treats diversity judgmentally	– treats diversity nonjudgmentally
– uses fear to create separation	– uses hope to create unity

We begin to see how the roots of co-dependency permeate the very fabric of our dominator model of society. It is in every institution, including our religious ones. Christianity, the prevailing Western religion, has been especially supportive of the dominator model. It uses hierarchy in its own system and also serves as a cultural police force for advancing and maintaining the dominator model.

The Influence of Christianity

Christianity was introduced to the world at a time when the worship of feminine values had already been pushed underground. Christ's message reflected a reverence for partnership models of relationship rather than for dominator models. For many of the people enslaved by Roman legions during that era, partnership was difficult to understand. This made it quite difficult for Jesus' contemporaries to recognize his true message, as quoted from Matthew 20:25-28.

> You know that the rulers of the gentiles dominate them, and their great men exercise authority over them. It shall not be so among you (Christians): But whoever would be great among you must be your servant, and whoever would be first among you must be your slave. Even as the son of man came not to be served but to serve, and to give his life as a ransom for many.

Christ's point was that leadership is a form of service to the whole. He recognized that when the lord adopts the role of the servant, both ranks or categories perish and a new order is instituted.

Jesus demonstrated this point graphically when he washed the feet of his disciples during the Last Supper. With this act he symbolized the demolition of a whole pattern of domination and submission, creating a partnership model for his religion.

Jesus also violated the rigidly male-dominated, sexually segregated norms of his times by associating freely with women, many of whom played major roles in early Christianity. At the same time, he preached what Eisler calls a partnership spirituality, elevating the so-called feminine values of compassion and nonviolence from their subservient place.

This partnership model of religion was not only preached but also practiced by many early Christians, some of whom were known as "Gnostics." These early Christians formed communities that were radically different from the rigidly male-dominated households, villages and cities of their times in that women and men worked and lived together in equal partnership. As Eisler notes, the important part played by women is perhaps reflected most dramatically in the Gnostic Gospels, banned as heretical by the orthodox church. These show that Mary Magdalene was probably the most important co-worker with Jesus of the Christian teachings.

These early Christians also practiced equal access to information, equal participation and equal claims to spiritual knowledge. They believed that each individual could make direct contact with the spiritual realms and that intermediaries such as priests, bishops and other hierarchical figures were unnecessary intrusions. At each worship, they drew lots to determine who carried out the priestly roles at that service. They did not confuse roles with the people who carried them out.

Various early sects of Christians eventually divided into two camps. The Orthodox Christians created a system based on hierarchy while others, including some of the Gnostics, created a non-hierarchical structure. These two groups came into conflict, with the Orthodox group eventually gaining power. Starting about 200 A.D., all references to the diety as both Mother and Father, were labeled heresy, and women were again officially excluded from the preisthood. The Orthodox group also ordered that all Gnostic writings be destroyed, beginning a long and vengeful campaign to wipe out Gnosticism and its challenge to the emerging male-dominated church and family. (Pagels 1979) This done, Christianity was well on its way to becoming precisely the kind of violent, hierarchical system against which Jesus had rebelled. Institutionalized Christianity, with its emphasis on male superiority, has helped to perpetuate a dominator model of society over the past 2000 years. (Eisler 1987)

Thus, one of the true messages of Christianity—partnership—was lost. The distorted teachings that remained were used to keep people powerless and hopeless. According to their Christian dogma, the average human being would never reach heaven without the priests, bishops and other intermediaries of the male-dominated church hierarchy. Those who intuitively sensed these teachings to be untrue and refused to follow the Church teachings were threatened with damnation to an eternal Hell. Women and men who remembered the teachings of the Great Goddess and the partnership model of spirituality were methodically persecuted. This persecution reached epidemic proportions by the Middle Ages, when it is estimated that over seven million women who had been judged as "witches" or heretics were killed or burned at the stake. (Starhawk 1979)

Whole villages identified with this demonic pagan religion were eradicated. This campaign was carried out with as much dedication and purposefulness as any world war we have ever had and certainly killed more people than any acknowledged war.

Many contemporary cultural historians such as José Argüelles (1987) recognize that this religious war continues and that now it has become a war against the Earth herself. Feminists such as Susan Griffin (1978) are looking at the parallels between the treatment of women and the treatment of the planet. The rise in domestic violence and rape parallels the rise in underground nuclear testing. The high incidence of hysterectomies among women parallels the increasing acceptance of the strip mining of coal and minerals. The attitude of seeing women as objects to be used and then cast aside has supported the emergence of a "disposable" society that throws away the planet's resources in the form of styrofoam, plastic, cardboard and paper as containers for food in the fast-food chains and processed food in the grocery stores. It is necessary for us to recognize the real causes of our cultural dysfunction so that we know how to begin to change it.

Co-dependent Systems

From this perspective we begin to see that the causes of co-dependency go right to the heart of our social structure. Any culture that ranks one sex over another, one religion over another or one race over another, has organized a society that is bound to be co-dependent. The dominator culture of the South during the Civil War era is an excellent example of a co-dependent society. The wealthy landowners managed their lives of ease and luxury, with black slaves providing the labor to fulfill their economic and personal needs. Most of the gentry were helpless in basic survival skills such as cooking, gardening and caring for their animals. The black people, by contrast, had basic survival skills but often lacked the ability to plan and manage. When the Emancipation Proclamation ended slavery, both groups discovered their areas of helplessness and co-dependency, which contributed to the eventual collapse of the whole system.

While co-dependency, *per se*, did not cause the fall of the South, a dominator structure with its values and beliefs was a major factor. Any system in which members are not encouraged to be self-reliant, self-directed and individually responsible creates passive people who are apathetic, helpless, fearful and unable to facilitate the changes that need to be made in the culture. This is evident in many authoritarian cultures, be they Eastern or Western, technologically developing or developed, ancient or modern. But it is still a major problem in our more democratic society today—with the basic obstacle to both personal and social health, systematically entrenched in the remaining orientation to the dominator model.

Using the dominator versus partnership model as a framework, let's explore how this affects our culture's economic system. Most of the economic systems of the Western world are based on some form of capitalism with an owner/worker structure. The owner sector (which includes stockholders as well as those with investments who do the actual managing) provides the risk-taking necessary to capitalize operations, assumes the responsibility for either success or failure and reaps any rewards. The owner sector has control of the entire venture, including who and when to hire and fire.

The worker sector, on the other hand, usually has little or no investment, no responsibility and very little financial risk. They provide the labor (negotiated at the owner's lowest possible price) so that the owner sector can make the highest profit possible. Workers, in return for their freedom from financial risk and responsibility, have little or no job security. At the mercy of the owners, workers keep their jobs based on how well the owners do. The owners survive only if the workers will work at the lowest possible wage. This is a clear case of a co-dependent relationship.

Co-dependency also exists in all the other Western institutions: medicine, education, religion, politics and the military. In medicine, physicians and therapists have assumed an authoritarian role as they seek to use their personal power to cure illness and disease. Patients are treated like some kind of a mechanical device with broken parts, with their body and mind kept separate. In the traditional medical system, the power is with the health-care provider. Patients (not clients) are treated as victims and encouraged to maintain positions of ignorance and powerlessness.

In education, a similar scenario has unfolded. Educational power is given to those who rank highest in the hierarchy. The student is the least regarded, least consulted component of the system. Most education is established by the culture and directed, delivered and evaluated by teachers. It assumes that students know little or nothing and forces them into compulsory attendance. The self-development, interests, needs and individual differences of the students are the least considered factors in creating an educational experience.

In religion, a hierarchy also maintains a system where the laity need priests, bishops, ministers and other clergy to structure and interpret their spiritual experience. The Catholic church, in particular, ranks priests over nuns (like doctors over nurses) in order to maintain patriarchal values.

Political systems rank people hierarchically according to power, particularly economic, racial and gender power. Western politics supports those who are rich, white and male, perpetuating a pervasive labor/management culture. We have essentially one political party, the Capitalist Party, which has liberal and conservative branches often called the Democratic and Republican parties. Both branches promote co-dependent structures and programs because capitalism, as it is practiced in this country, is a dominator model.

The use of military power provides a method for enforcing the dominator model. It supports the life-taking, destructive values that help to keep people mistrustful, fearful and separate.

Each of these institutions, though different in function, is supported by the principles of the dominator model. If we begin to examine our basic patterns of relating in our intimate relationships, we can see that our patterns of relating must change at every level of the culture. Such changes will cause a radical shift in the way that we see ourselves and the way we view our world. This is the kind of shift that Peter Russell (1983) and Theodore Roszak (1979) describe as a "shift in consciousness."

The Consciousness Revolution: The Why Behind the Co-dependency Epidemic

Our clients frequently ask us why there is such an epidemic of co-dependency, wondering why all the furor over something that seemed to work for their parents and their grandparents. Our response to this is "increasing awareness." In the last twenty-five years there has been a virtual explosion of information and knowledge about us as human beings—about our brains, our development and about the universe in which we live. Much of this information has come as the result of what is called "the human potential" movement.

This movement has revealed, for the first time in modern history, the astounding nature of human capacities. A few scientists and researchers, working independently at first, eventually grew into a network of people from science, religion, philosophy and education who are creating a new picture of human possibilities. This new human:

- has 900% more physical and mental abilities (based on the premise that we use only about 10% of it today) (Houston 1982)

- is able to learn and think in multiple ways (visually in symbols, kinesthetically with the body, sensorially with feelings and auditorially with words)

- has 200 or more senses, many of which come from cross-sensing (such as tasting colors) (Houston 1982)

- is able to shift into different brain wave frequencies at will, consciously altering states of awareness

- is able to create and direct his or her own destiny through the thoughts or images that are generated internally

- is able to heal himself or herself of what have been considered "terminal" illnesses through the use of meditation, nutrition, affirmations, psychotherapy and exercise

- is capable of being "self-aware," that is, aware of being aware.

The release of this new view about human possibilities began in the 1960s just as many people were feeling their loss of personal freedom and were recognizing the degree of their dependence on large social and governmental systems. People began to experience a yearning for growth, for greater opportunities, for authenticity and for self-determination. There arose a movement for self-development, for values that support the fullest unfoldment of the potential of human beings. Imbedded in this human potential movement was a growing awareness of how traditional childbirth, parenting, families and the educational system can interfere with the development of our full humanness.

Psychologists began to investigate the sources of emotional trauma in both adults and children and also to explore these new ideas about human possibilities. In researching these two things simultaneously, the psychologists began to see patterns of relationship between the quality of child-rearing practices and the level of potential people were able to achieve. It became clear that the way our culture has parented its children has interfered with the development of their human capacities. Most of us, it seems, have gotten stuck in early phases of our developmental programming and are unable to move toward wholeness and psychological independence. The awareness of how our culturally based parenting practices make it difficult to complete important stages of human development during childhood and consequently reduce human capacities has caused a critical awakening of consciousness. This awakening requires that we look more closely at the process of human development so that we understand its stages, challenges, tasks and, also, the pitfalls. The next chapter takes a closer look at this process and offers a developmental approach to recovery.

CHAPTER FOUR

A Developmental Approach to Recovery

The developmental approach to recovery presented in this book views co-dependency as a developmental problem that involves the whole family system. It is caused by a failure to complete certain crucial developmental tasks—particularly bonding and separation—during the first six years of life.

If something happens to disrupt the completion of either of these tasks, they will continue to recycle during life, trying to find completion. The result of incomplete bonding and/or separateness is co-dependency. A co-dependent person will get "stuck" in (1) trying to complete bonding by becoming very attached or dependent or (2) trying to complete separation or autonomy by being very unattached or counter-dependent or (3) cycling back and forth between the two.

Almost all the research on early child development has to be reassessed because it focuses almost exclusively on the mother/child relationship. Only recently (Mahler 1968) has the role of the father been studied and then only as it relates to the separation process in child development. Little is known about the role of the father in the bonding process. This is not surprising considering that the dominator model does not support partnership parenting, leaving the bonding and separation tasks to the mother and child.

The next two chapters will present a developmental approach to co-dependency, looking first at the principles that support this kind of approach and then at the normal course of development during early childhood. Finally, we will look at where the developmental process breaks down, leaving people stuck in the co-dependency trap.

MAIN PRINCIPLES OF A DEVELOPMENTAL APPROACH

In a developmental approach, painful and anxiety-producing events in life are seen as developmental crises rather than as emotional breakdowns or mental illnesses. This approach uses a number of key principles that help us understand the causes of co-dependency:

• All development is a continuous process from conception until death. It is sequential, in that one task helps provide the foundation for the next one.

• Any developmental task that isn't mastered at the age-appropriate time is carried along as excess baggage into subsequent developmental stages. If too many tasks are not completed on schedule, the developmental process can become overloaded and break down.

• Incomplete developmental tasks will press for completion whenever they can. Any situation that resembles an earlier situation where the incompleted developmental task was involved will bring the unresolved issue to the forefront. People report being flooded by old feelings or old memories. They feel "rubberbanded" back into the original emotional experience when they were first trying to complete the task.

• When people realize that incomplete developmental tasks are the cause of their overreactions to certain people or situations, they are able to learn new, more effective responses. Through increased awareness of the causes of the problems and through increased communication skills, people can bring previously incomplete developmental tasks to completion.

Four Stages of Relationship

In this approach to recovery, co-dependency is seen as the first stage of a four-stage process of personal development that should be completed by age twelve. Ideally, the process should occur in the following way.

When we are born, we are already in the first stage: co-dependency. Nature provides a symbiotic relationship between child and mother in which neither experiences separation between them. This is nature's way of insuring that the human infant will get the care it needs to survive. Mother and child live together in a fused or enmeshed atmosphere of unity and oneness, working on the primary tasks of bonding and creating trust. This stage lasts about six to nine months until the child begins to creep and crawl.

Stage two of the process is counter-dependency. During this period, which peaks at about eighteen to thirty-six months of age, the primary developmental task is separation. By this time, both parents and child have strong needs to become more independent people. The child has a strong drive to explore the world and be separate ("I want to do it myself."), while the parents yearn to spend more time on their long-term interests such as their careers and their relationship. The separation process, which occurs gradually over a period of two to three years, is discussed in detail in Chapter Five.

If stage two is completed without any problems, then, by about age three, the child is ready to move into stage three: independence. During this stage, which usually lasts until age six, the child is able to function autonomously much of the time and still feels and acts related to his or her parents and family.

Upon completion of stage three, the child is ready to move into the fourth stage of relationship: interdependence. In this last stage, which usually occurs between ages six and twelve, the degree of relationship between the child and others fluctuates. At times she or he may wish to be close and at other times may wish to be more separate. The primary task of this stage is being able to move back and forth comfortably between oneness and separateness.

Main Developmental Tasks of Early Childhood

While bonding and separateness are the two main developmental tasks of children during the period from birth to three years and three years to six years, there are other important developmental tasks as well. They are listed below.

Birth to Three Years

- Bonding with mother, father and significant others
- Developing a sense of basic trust
- Learning to feed oneself and to eat a variety of foods
- Learning to manipulate simple objects and to explore the environment safely
- Learning to walk and talk
- Learning to control elimination
- Learning to defer gratification
- Learning to handle frustration

Three to Six Years

- Bonding with the Earth
- Developing a sense of self, separate from others

- Developing object constancy; that is, the ability to hold onto self as an object of worth, even when facing defeat or criticism

- Developing the ability to take responsibility for actions and decisions

- Developing the ability to share with others

- Learning to manage frustration and aggressive tendencies in constructive ways

- Learning to identify feelings in self and others

- Learning to follow oral instructions

- Learning to be reasonably independent in daily functions (washing, dressing, toilet training, eating)

- Developing realistic concepts of the physical and social world (time, space, distance, authority)

- Learning appropriate sex role identifications

Bonding: The Critical Task of Co-dependency

The critical developmental task of co-dependency between mother and child is bonding, which allows for basic trust to develop. If anything happens to interfere with the bonding process, the child may get stuck in co-dependency and also have difficulty in trusting.

A newborn baby, if permitted to do so, bonds almost immediately to his or her mother and father. The sound of both parents' voices, the sight of their faces during holding or feeding, the feel of their skin and the smell of their bodies are constant signals for the child that there is some order and consistency to this seemingly chaotic and confusing world.

Researchers Klaus and Kennell (1976) have contributed much to our understanding of the bonding process. Their findings are summarized below:

- The optimal period for bonding is from the first few minutes after birth through the first twelve to twenty-four hours.

During that time they suggest that both parents spend a significant amount of time having skin-to-skin and other sensory contact with their child.

- The parents have to receive signals that the child is responding to their attempts to bond. Otherwise they may get discouraged and withdraw from their baby, making bonding more difficult.

- Everyone present during the birth process will likely have some bonding to the child. This suggests that immediate and extended family members should be allowed to be present at the birth of the child.

- A newborn with a life-threatening illness will be difficult for the parents to bond to. Parents will hold back and fear the feelings of loss they would have to deal with should the child die. Also, fathers have trouble bonding with the child if their wife has any life-threatening complications during the birth process. Fathers who are not present at their child's birth also may have more trouble bonding with their child.

- Any emotional conflict of the parents that causes them to be tense or worried during the first few hours after birth can have long-term effects on the child's development.

- Even if the optimal period of bonding is disrupted by illness, bonding can occur subsequently if the parents continue to establish sensory contact with the child whenever possible.

It appears from the research of Mahler (1968) and her colleagues that the child's ability to achieve autonomy or separateness at age two or three is somewhat dependent on the completion of the earlier developmental task of bonding. The more completely the child bonds to the mother and father during the first days and months of life, the easier it is for the child and the parents to successfully work through and complete the separation process. A mother or father who is not fully bonded to their child is more likely to neglect or abuse that child than a mother or father who completed the bonding process with their child. A child who doesn't fully bond with her or his father or mother will become attached instead. Attached children behave differently from bonded children. They are afraid of the world and they fear change. They approach others with timidity and caution that make exploring the unknown a much more difficult task. They need concrete, overt, physical signals such as touch or very specific sensory directions to guide their actions. These children have difficulty in perceiving subtle or intuitive signals, so they tend to react to situations rather than to anticipate them. Attached people, in order to compensate for their lack of bonding, close off their feelings, become rigid in their thinking and eventually develop compulsive behaviors that they use to numb or quiet the increasing sense of anxiety about the uncertainty of their life.

By contrast, children who are more fully bonded are not afraid to explore their world and they delight in novelty and change. They approach others with receptivity and an openness to learning. They can pick up on subtle and intuitive signals that allow them to be spontaneous and relaxed. These children are often aptly described as having a love affair with the world. (Greenacre 1958)

Separation: The Critical Task of Counter-dependency

Mahler's (1968) research is useful in charting the course of development of separateness. She found four distinct sub-stages in this process:

1) differentiation

2) early practicing

3) rapprochement

4) object constancy.

During the differentiation sub-stage (five months to eleven months), the child begins to see himself/herself as separate from mother or father. At first this occurs in very small ways. The child explores mother's or father's face, grabbing at their noses and ears or pulling to the edge of their laps to see the world out there. Then the child starts to creep and crawl, but always in sight or earshot of mother or father.

In the second sub-stage (ten to sixteen months), the child begins to stand upright and eventually to walk. This allows her or him to explore farther and farther away from mother or father. Parents soon find that their child can climb to incredible heights and can roam at unbelievable distances in an attempt to explore his/her world. A child needs to be met with at least twice as many "yeses" as "nos" during this stage. The environment needs to be "kid proofed," rather than restricting the child's movements, in order for him or her to develop optimal exploratory behaviors in relative safety.

The third sub-stage (fifteen months to two years) is marked by a rediscovery of mother and father, now as more separate individuals, and by returning to them after being out exploring the world. A child begins to realize her or his separateness and feels scared and vulnerable. The child may shadow her or his father or mother, not letting them out of sight. Also, a battle of wills begins and he or she starts demanding the father's or mother's attention or presence. Angry outbursts and temper tantrums mark this period, although these can begin earlier. A temper tantrum is a release of frustration and tension from the body. Once it is over, the child feels peaceful and calm inside and is ready to forgive and be forgiven. A reassuring hug from a parent that tells the child he or she is still loved is all that is necessary. Most parents get caught up in what seems like a battle of wills and find it hard to simply forgive and forget.

The fourth sub-stage (two years to three years) requires the child to learn to reconcile her or his intense longings for the bliss of oneness with an equally intense need for separateness and individual selfhood. This eventually precipitates the developmental crisis of the psychological birth. These conflicting forces battling inside a child can only be resolved through object constancy: the ability to see self and other as separate objects with both good and bad qualities. When the child ventures too far away and gets afraid, or falls and bumps an elbow or knee, the child expects mother or father to be right there to provide comfort.

Without the full development of "object constancy," a child sees the parent as "good parent" when he or she is available and as "bad parent" when he or she is not available. They essentially split the world into good and bad. A three-year-old child should have developed enough object constancy to hold on to a positive image of the mother or father while away from them at pre-school or visiting friends. Children may long for the presence of their parent, but they do not fantasize that their parents are bad or have abandoned them and no longer love them. Three-year-olds need to have built up enough "good parent" and "good self" experiences to allow themselves to function separately from their parents. Children can even have angry or hateful thoughts toward their parents or themselves and not be overwhelmed by these feelings.

The reconciliation of this "good parent/bad parent" splitting is essential for the completion of the psychological birth. In addition to an adequate amount of object constancy, reconciliation seems to require the presence of a nurturing father or mother who can help provide a buffer for the child when the other parent simply is not available. Sensitive, nurturing parents can help children differentiate themselves from either their mother or father, maleness from femaleness, and masculine from feminine.

Both parents must take an active role in the whole process. They must be present at the beginning so bonding with father can occur as well as with mother. At the time of the psychological birth, the role of the parents is to provide some nurturing support for the child and at the same time provide nurturing support for each other.

When the Process Breaks Down

There are several critical places in both the bonding process and the separateness process where things can break down. In the bonding process it is important that, immediately after the child's birth, both parents get maximum skin-to-skin contact with their child. It is important that the father bond to the child so that he can eventually support the separation process when it begins later. If the child is separated from his or her mother or father during the period of 12-24 hours following birth, the optimal time for bonding is missed. Bonding certainly can and does occur after that optimal time, but it requires more effort on the part of the parents to supply the necessary sensory contact.

Another critical factor in these two early stages is the degree to which the mother and father have completed their own issues of oneness and separateness. Most of us were raised by parents who never completed the bonding and/or separation process themselves. As a result, they were unable to provide us with the support, information and skills needed to complete this important developmental task on schedule. That is why at least 98% of our population have symptoms of co-dependency. Parents who never completed their own separation process have both a fear of closeness and a fear of separation. Their fear of closeness may create anxiety that they will be engulfed by their child and lose their own somewhat fragile sense of separateness. On the other hand, their fear of separation may arise when their child pulls away to become a separate, autonomous person. Both of these things frequently happen between child and parent. These two conflicting sets of needs and fears cause parents to send out conflicting messages to their children, often interfering with the normal developmental process.

It is important once the parents have bonded to the child that they both be physically and emotionally present for the child during the separation stage. Their presence and the support they provide throughout the first several years of a child's life are critical in the completion of the separation process so that the child does not get stuck in co-dependency.

Case Example

Madeline came to me (Barry) complaining of a rather bizarre set of physical symptoms for which her physician could find no cause. She had an intense burning in her chest, a loss of hearing, dizziness, constipation and skin rashes. She also reported having very co-dependent, conflictual relationships. As she related her personal history, I found out that she had been physically and sexually abused as a child. Her mother beat her, and her father raped her during a drunken episode and then left the family.

She had believed that she was such a bad person that she caused her father to leave. Her mother had actually told her that. Finally, I asked her about her birth. From what she had learned, her mother suffered complications during delivery and almost died. She learned that it had been two weeks before her mother actually saw her for the first time. She also learned that her father came to see only his wife during this two-week period. He was unable to face the possibility of his wife dying and the possibility of having to raise a child alone. The lack of parental bonding with Madeline certainly contributed to their physical and sexual abuse of her.

My work with her involved both bonding and separateness issues. Initially, we worked on bonding and building trust. Then I began to help her separate herself from me and from her mother. At first, she was so identified with her mother that she told me that when she looked in the mirror, she saw her mother, not herself. I asked her to list all the positive and negative ways she was like her mother and all the positive and negative ways she was *not* like her mother. In her first list, she listed mostly the positive ways she was like her mother ("We have the same smile") and a few negative ways ("We both hate ourselves"), but she could not think of one way she was different from her mother. Each time we met, I encouraged her to come up with at least one way she was different from her mother. Gradually she began to build a positive self-image that was separate from her mother. The more she was able to see herself as separate from her mother, the more her physical symptoms disappeared. Madeline will have to work hard to maintain object constancy, but she gained some valuable tools in therapy to continue working to break her co-dependency in relationships.

Summary

This chapter has presented information on a developmental view of how co-dependency forms. An understanding of the process of how co-dependency is created is essential to full recovery from this developmental disorder. This approach emphasizes that once you understand how co-dependency is created, it is possible to break free of the trap in which you find yourself.

CHAPTER FIVE

The Causes of Co-dependency

The Role of the Father

For the psychological birth to be completed successfully around age two or three, it is necessary for both parents to act as a buffer between the child and the other parent during the separation process. It is this parental support that helps the child complete the differentiation process—to know self from other and to begin to think in ways that recognize both good and bad qualities in himself or herself and others. Unfortunately, our dominator culture hasn't provided either appropriate models or adequate information on the role of both parents. So neither knows how to be an effective, supportive parent in this process. With the breaking of rigid cultural roles since the 1960s, however, more and more parents are learning about partnership parenting and about how to help their children complete this process successfully.

There are several things that either parent does, as a result of our dominator culture, that can interfere with separation and differentiation. For example, the father may teach girls that they need to be rescued by men and may encourage boys to devalue women and overvalue men. Also, fathers often get scared about being in the middle of what seems like a battle of wills between mother and child, and they withdraw into work or other activities that take them out of the picture. Some fathers get so frightened that they even leave the relationship completely rather than be drawn into the power struggle. A dependent mother can also feel threatened that the child's father will try to drive a wedge between mother and child, and she may try to force a weak father out of the home at this stage. This leaves mother and child to fend for themselves and, as a result, the likelihood of the psychological birth getting completed is reduced to almost zero.

Emotional constancy survives only in the context of relationship. For instance, if children are left alone to fend for themselves at this crucial point and are not given emotional support, they will choose to remain dependent on their parents rather than risk separateness. They will likely settle for a belief that they are not okay and cannot survive without the care and protection of their parents. They will then stay focused on external rewards and begin to turn away from their own inner desires and feelings.

What is required for children to achieve separation from their parents is the loving presence of a father or mother or two bonded care-givers who are secure enough in their own "selfhood" to risk being in the middle of the struggle for a while. They must have empathy for both each other and their child and also be able to extend tenderness to them during these maddening months. Without this, children are unable to become emotionally separate enough to see their parents as separate objects with both good and bad qualities and also to see themselves as a separate object with good and bad qualities.

Object Constancy

If there isn't enough object constancy present in children when they see their mother or father as "bad parent," then they will see themselves as "bad child" as well. There is no differentiation. *No one ever achieves separateness or autonomy by making the other person bad or wrong.* Many people try to separate from their parents as teenagers or later as adults by using this approach. Separateness comes only from a perspective of seeing both the good and the bad in your mother or father and yourself. ("You're okay and so am I").

If there *is* enough object constancy available, you learn to accept the idea that no human being is perfectly good or absolutely evil. You can accept the imperfections of your loved ones and yourself and still hold on to your "goodness" even when your personal demons seem to torment you the most. You can tolerate your mixed feelings toward others and see them as whole human beings with both vices and virtues. Also, you are able to do the same for yourself and need not cast out parts of yourself that you don't like very much. You can take responsibility for your conflicting behaviors, feelings and thoughts and not have to project them onto others.

If you haven't developed enough object constancy, you cannot reconcile the contradictions between oneness and separateness, and you will fail in repeated attempts to complete your psychological birth. You will probably regulate your life by splitting your experiences into the irreconcilable dichotomies of all-good and all-bad. Your thinking will be dominated by comparisons. You will see yourself as better or worse than others. You will feel either "one-up" or "one-down" in relationships and have trouble feeling like an equal with anyone.

You will feel in control only when you can manipulate another into becoming the supportive, all-giving partner who will help sustain your own image of self-perfection (all good). You may temporarily idealize these partners. Eventually, however, your partner will want to be just an ordinary person with needs and wants of his or her own. This partner will be unable to grant magical wishes or be a person who refuses to allow his or her comings and goings to be controlled.

At this point the unavailable partner often is seen as all bad and is devalued is some way. ("I'll show you I don't need you.") Frustration and disappointment can erupt into rage and fury if your partner suddenly becomes too independent. However, the expression of this rage may drive the partner further away, so you may not risk the full expression of rage when you are in a needy situation. Therefore, a safer course is often chosen. This may involve manipulating your partner into some perceived blunder so you can be justifiably angry at them and discharge your pent-up feelings. However, there is an even better way to control your partner.

The Replay in Adult Relationships

If you can make your partner dependent upon you, then he or she can't stray too far away. If he or she does, you can pull them back by doing things you know you can do for them that they believe they can't do for themselves. This keeps the relationship in a state where each controls the other through co-dependency. Husbands often make their wives dependent by controlling the family finances, while wives make their husbands dependent by taking care of their personal needs, such as laundry and cooking. It often doesn't occur to either one to share what they know with the other, for fear of breaking out of the co-dependency trap. Because this is not negotiated in a direct manner, it becomes a way of controlling each other rather than a way to cooperate with each other.

The Drama Triangle

What really keeps the co-dependency trap constantly sprung is the Drama Triangle. (Karpman 1968) A co-dependent person frequently feels "victimized" by the unwillingness of his or her partner to help create the ideal relationship where all their needs will be anticipated and met. As a result, they feel they have to create a way to be a victim in the relationship to get their needs met without having to ask for them. Enter the Drama Triangle. The first act of the drama usually starts with an interaction between the persecutor and the victim. The second act begins when the rescuer comes to save the victim. In the third act, the rescuer attacks the persecutor. Then a new drama begins. The persecutor becomes the victim, the rescuer becomes the persecutor and the victim moves into the rescuer position. These unfolding dramas work like a merry-go-round, with the players rotating positions. What keeps the merry-go-round going is competition for the victim position.

For example, if father has had a bad day at work, he might act as the persecutor by yelling at the kids for making too much noise when he gets home. They feel like victims and they complain to mother about father. Mother then rescues them by telling them that their father didn't mean what he said. Then she becomes a persecutor because she feels her peaceful home has been disturbed and starts criticizing her husband for yelling at the children. This causes father to exclaim, "I get chewed out at work and then come home and get chewed out by you." He may either collapse in a heap as the true victim he feels like, or he may get competition for the victim position from his wife who now says, "I was only trying to help things. I sit home all day while you go out and be with other people. I get bored and am tired of being treated this way." They may then get into a fight about who has it worse until the kids come to the rescue by saying, "Don't fight; we will be quiet." Depending on the relative strength of each individual's need to be a victim, this game could go on all evening with endless variations.

You will notice in the Drama Triangle that there is a relationship between the persecutor and the victim and between the victim and the rescuer. There is no relationship, however, between the rescuer and the persecutor. This lack of relationship is critical, for if the rescuer and the persecutor stopped to communicate, the game would be over. We believe that the Drama Triangle is an attempt to complete the mother/father/child relationship in the counter-dependency stage. Because we haven't fully understood the role of each parent in supporting the child in completing the separation process, our relationship patterns have gotten stuck in the dysfunctional triangle.

You can easily spot Drama Triangle games because they frequently involve people complaining about each other without asking directly for what they want. People attempt to make others feel guilty for not giving them something they want, usually by complaining a lot about the behavior of others. Or they use other indirect means, such as manipulating the other person into giving them what they want without ever asking for it.

While the persecutor role and the victim role are often easier to identify, the rescuer role requires further definition. Rescuing is doing something for someone else that they could actually do for themselves. It is a "one-up" move that puts someone down. Doing something for someone that they could do for themselves without them asking for it or without you asking them for permission is a power play. It is an invasion of the other person's space that comes from the position, "I'm only trying to help you." It is a subtle way to control others and undermine their self-esteem. In alcoholic families, these people are known as "enablers" and "caretakers." People in the helping professions can easily fall into being rescuers if they are not careful. Remember, the ultimate goal of this game is to get to be a victim. Rescuers will often get themselves persecuted so that they can have a turn in the victim role. For example, they might unconsciously fail to offer someone just the right kind of help. A rescuer may also try to help someone who doesn't want help so that they can be rejected. Then they can feel hurt and become the victim.

Case Example

Ed and Lucille had been married twenty-three years when they came to us for counseling. The last of their children was about to leave home and Lucille was beginning to feel the "empty nest" syndrome. The primary complaint about the relationship came from Lucille, who was wanting more intimacy with Ed. Without the children around, Lucille found herself with more time on her hands. Her usual routine of cleaning, shopping, doing laundry and attending school activities had been reduced to nearly nothing. Because of her devotion to the children and their interests and to supporting Ed in his corporate career, she had not developed many personal interests or relationships. Her home and family had been her profession.

Ed, on the other hand, had not had much involvement in the family. His business commitments required him to travel frequently and to work long hours. He had grown up as an only child in an emotionally distant family with parents who had not married until their late thirties. Ed learned quite early in life to play quietly and entertain himself. While he knew his parents loved him, he never felt close to either of them.

In working with Ed and Lucille, it became obvious that Lucille was quite co-dependent and Ed quite counter-dependent. Though Lucille recognized her co-dependency, she was surprised to learn that Ed was counter-dependent. She had always imagined him as a warm and loving partner who expressed his mutual devotion by providing well for the family. She tended not to see his detachment or his need for isolation, which was easy for her to overlook with her great devotion to the children and her home.

We were able to help them see their very different patterns of relationship and how they had been able to make them work as long as they had with the children to distract them and camouflage the issues. With the children gone, Lucille needed someone else to whom to attach herself. This need was creating a great deal of difficulty for Ed, who was experiencing Lucille's attachment as an invasion of his psychological space.

He had become quite uncomfortable with Lucille's desire for a closer relationship and wanted Lucille to find a job or something to keep her occupied. He really was not eager to form a closer relationship with Lucille. This left Lucille with a number of options. She could persist in trying to pull Ed closer. She could explore fulfilling her need for attachment through work or personal friendships. Or she could even explore whether she wanted to stay in her relationship with Ed. This is where therapy with Ed and Lucille stopped, as Lucille explored her options.

Summary

Relationships with one co-dependent and one counter-dependent partner are very common. A person with emotionally distant parents often marries a person who is more dependent and attached, while a person with dependent and attached parents will seek a mate who is more detached. This attraction to opposites is an attempt to resolve the unfinished early childhood issues of bonding and separation. "Opposites" relationships, however, often have more conflict as these early issues recycle frequently and press for completion. The conflict is usually a replay of the conflict experienced with either parent and needs to be framed as an opportunity for growth rather than as dysfunctional behavior.

Part Two

THE RECOVERY PROCESS

CHAPTER SIX

The Elements of Recovery

This section of the book will focus on the process of recovery from co-dependency. The main theme of this section is that *full recovery from co-dependency is possible*. The resources necessary for recovery are a willingness to change, the courage to look at your life in new ways and a willingness to ask for help from others.

THE ELEMENTS OF RECOVERY

The healing elements that seem to hold the most promise for helping you break out of co-dependency are:

- your willingness and ability to work on yourself alone, without your partner, your therapist or your support group
- committed, conscious, cooperative relationships
- a therapist who understands co-dependency, who has

worked through it personally, and who knows how to treat it

• groups, classes and workshops where you can get the support of others who are serious about changing their co-dependent patterns.

Your willingness to work on yourself alone is the most critical element. It is easy for a co-dependent person to turn the responsibility for their healing over to someone else who they assume knows more than they do. Partners, therapists and support groups can inadvertently support co-dependency while working on the cure.

Finally, this section of the book presents a 12-step process of recovery that expands upon the 12-step processes that many people have used to deal with other addictions like alcohol, eating, drugs, etc. This process contains the essential steps for full recovery from co-dependency.

Working On Yourself Alone

No other healing element has the same power as your own work on yourself. This book and other books frequently offer awareness activities that can be done by yourself. These activities can help you learn more about yourself and your co-dependency.

Completing written exercises is one common way of working on yourself alone. This can include filling out questionnaires or inventories to help you identify your problems more clearly. Keeping a journal or diary on a regular basis can also be a big help to locate patterns over time. Art, dance or other expressive methods can also be very helpful.

There are other individual processes that can be very useful in building higher self-esteem. One of these is breath work, which helps clear negative patterns of disease and tension that are lodged in the body. More information on how to use this tool is given at the end of Chapter Fourteen. Another powerful individual tool is "mirror work." Learning to love yourself involves being able to sit in front of a mirror and say loving things to yourself. More information on this tool is given in Chapter Fifteen. Both of these tools can be combined with affirmations, which are highly positive self-statements that can be written or repeated verbally. Affirmations are recognized as an effective way to change self-limiting beliefs and perceptions, which are very common among co-dependents.

Each chapter that describes one of the steps of recovery will offer specific tools that can be used to work through that step. The tools will be divided into categories. Some will be for committed relationships, some to use as a client in therapy, others to use in support groups and some for working on yourself alone. The majority of the tools presented will be most useful as you work on yourself alone or with a partner.

Choosing a Therapist Who Understands

Psychotherapy can provide an important healing element in the recovery process. People with co-dependent patterns may find themselves repeating these patterns over and over again and finally decide to seek therapy to help them understand why these self-defeating patterns are so persistent. They realize that they can't figure it out by themselves and need someone more objective to help them unravel the mysteries of their adult life.

The most important thing about therapy is finding the right therapist. You should start by looking for someone who has done his or her own personal work. Not all therapists have broken their own co-dependent patterns. If they haven't gotten clear of their patterns, they may tend to try to recreate co-dependent relationships with their clients. Ask your therapist about his or her co-dependent patterns and how he or she has dealt with them. If you get answers like, "That's none of your business," or "I'm the therapist and I ask the questions," you may want to choose another therapist.

A therapist who is consciously working to overcome his or her own co-dependent tendencies (Remember: 98% of the population, including therapists, are co-dependent) can be a valuable model as well as a source of practical help in breaking co-dependency. This kind of therapist will be interested in helping a client to expand his/her views of himself/herself and in teaching him/her how to look at his/her behavior from an expanded view of possibilities. They will be careful not to rescue their clients, and they will help their clients to assume more and more responsibility for their own lives.

Support Groups, Classes and Workshops

When you are in the process of breaking out of the co-dependency trap, you may assume that you are the only one going through the problems you are experiencing. Support groups containing other people who are facing the same problems you are facing can provide a broader perspective to your problem and perhaps offer a variety of possible solutions from which to choose. Many support groups in the addictions field are based primarily on the Alcoholics Anonymous 12-step model. Groups such as these are often a place to begin if you are not sure about how to spot your co-dependent patterns.

For co-dependents, there are Adult Children of Alcoholics (ACOA) support groups and Co-Dependents Anonymous (CoDA) groups. Co-Dependents Anonymous groups are usually run very informally. People don't have to identify their last names or where they work. They don't even have to say anything if they don't want to. They don't have to pay money, except for a donation to cover coffee and room rentals if they want to. No one has to sign up or register or answer questions. They just have to attend, and by their presence at the meeting they are admitting they have co-dependent patterns.

Meeting formats vary with each group. Some groups have no leader for the evening and anyone can talk or discuss feelings and problems. Other groups have a designated leader who may talk about a personal problem and relate it to one of the Steps. Sometimes groups select a theme around one of the Steps, and anybody who wishes can comment on that theme as it applies to them. Sometimes homework is suggested for those who are interested in going further with the theme. Usually an informal network develops so people call each other when they need support.

Many courses and workshops on co-dependency are being offered to the general public. Churches, schools, mental health groups and civic organizations often sponsor these classes, and the price is usually very reasonable. These can give co-dependents lots of information on the nature of the problem and help them meet others who are working on co-dependency.

The Three C's—Committed, Conscious and Cooperative Relationships

The last healing source is through relationships, if they have a high degree of commitment, consciousness and cooperation. Such relationships may come in many forms, such as between friends, business partners, parents and children, or as a couple.

Commitment can be defined in many ways. For our purposes, the most common aspects of commitment include:

- a willingness of both people to stay with the relationship and not run away from the problems

- a willingness of both people to change

- a willingness of both people to be emotionally honest.

Consciousness refers to the degree to which people are aware of their behavior and can begin to understand what motivates them to do what they do. Cooperation means a willingness to help each other in the healing process. Many co-dependent relationships are competitive rather than cooperative in nature. In a cooperative relationship, people freely teach and learn from each other instead of withholding information or using it to manipulate and control their partner.

A conscious, committed relationship can provide a strong therapeutic context for people who wish to break out of the co-dependency trap. It provides the arena where old patterns can be broken and new patterns can be developed. This is love and intimacy at its highest and best. Most people are likely to define intimacy as only those warm, close, maybe sexual times that are all blissful and serene.

The definition of intimacy has to be expanded to include those times when you are struggling to get free of old co-dependent patterns and your partner is right there with you, supporting you and loving you in your vulnerability, sadness, anger or pain. This is the kind of intimacy that helps you heal your wounds and "whole" your spirit. Many people are discovering who they really are and who their partner of many years really is. This can be an exciting adventure that opens you to the depths of human love and intimacy.

No therapist or support group can provide enough of the necessary rebonding required to break co-dependency. In committed relationships of any kind, the individuals often have to rebond to each other and then break the bonds in a straight, clean and healthy way, which is how the psychological birth finally gets completed.

A New 12-Step Process of Recovery

Recovery from co-dependency is a process that has some predictable steps in it. The order of these steps will likely be different with each individual, but it seems necessary to "touch all the bases" before returning home, free from co-dependent patterns. Some people will need to do much more than "touch the base" of some of the steps. For example, the first step, which involves recognizing the extent of the co-dependent patterns in your relationships, can take considerable time and effort. What makes it so difficult is that co-dependency is so pervasive that you may not recognize it as dysfunctional behavior. As a friend of ours said when we described a co-dependent pattern, "What's wrong with that? Isn't that the way everybody acts?" Other steps also can require intensive work. Learning to feel your feelings more fully and learning how to express your feelings in effective ways usually requires lots of hard work.

Recognizing Co-dependent Patterns. There are lots of ways to avoid recognizing the existence of co-dependency. It's like being asleep. You dream that things are one way. Even if they aren't that way, you keep dreaming. Because almost everything you have been exposed to has co-dependent overtones, you may not be aware that there is something better.

For some of you, denial may have been a learned survival or safety mechanism. If you really saw or talked about what was happening in your family where you grew up, you might not have survived childhood. You may have been taught not to notice what was happening to you and to other people in your family in order to maintain a "one big happy family" fantasy for the outside world. Of all the things you were taught to ignore, it is the lack of recognition of your own feelings that usually has the most devastating effects on you and your relationships. Co-dependency, like most addictions, is a feeling disorder.

Understanding the Causes of the Problem. There is much confusion in the literature about the actual causes of co-dependency. Some claim it is the result of a genetic weakness, while others claim it comes from contact with alcoholics or an alcoholic family. The main thesis of this book is that it is caused by a developmental flaw and it is learned dysfunctional behavior. It is also seen as a systemic problem related to growing up in a dysfunctional family and a dysfunctional society.

Unraveling Co-dependent Relationships. Once you understand that the causes of co-dependency originate in relationship dynamics that never got completed, you can begin to see how those dynamics recycle in your present relationships. The completion of your psychological birth process is the dynamic that is pressing for recognition all the time in co-dependent relationships. When you learn to recognize what you left undone, then, with additional support and new skills, you can consciously finish the process.

Taking Back Your Projections. When you attempt to become separate by making others wrong or bad, you usually develop a lifestyle based on projection. You may twist reality to suit your need to be right and justify your behavior by making others wrong. Taking back these projections often requires the loving confrontation and support of group or family members, friends and partners, a spouse or a therapist. Projections are the building blocks in the wall of denial. They tend to fall away slowly until enough of the wall of denial is removed and the truth of who you and others are is finally revealed.

Eliminating Self-Hate. If you didn't become separate from your mother or your family and you tried to separate by making them wrong or bad, you will likely end up making yourself wrong or bad as well. You may try to deny or cover up these negative feelings, but they usually run your life. It is necessary to uncover, claim and transform these negative images. They are based on misperceptions and illusions and are also the result of poor object constancy. By understanding that these projections are the source of your low self-esteem, you can correct them.

Eliminating Power Plays and Manipulation. Lacking the full natural power that comes from the completion of the psychological birth, you are likely to utilize power plays and manipulations to get what you want. The drama triangle (persecutor, rescuer and victim roles) is a common way to manipulate others while remaining very passive. As you find more effective ways to get people to cooperate with you, the need to try to control others will drop away.

Asking For What You Want. One of the most simple, straightforward ways to get what you want is to ask for it directly in such a way that people are delighted to give it to you (if they have it to give). What usually happens is that people don't ask directly ("I might be needing the car later.") and then get disappointed when people don't rescue them, or they ask with so much anger or resentment ("Damn it, I've got to have the car tonight! Can I have it?") that the other person resists and says no.

Learning to Feel Again. Children raised in dysfunctional families learn very early to deny their feelings and thoughts about what is happening in their home. One of the most frequently denied feelings is anger, even though people in co-dependent relationships are angry much of the time. Anger has to be "justified" in some way before it can be expressed. Someone has to be blamed or made the scapegoat for all the unhappiness in the family. Children often are used in this way. As an adult, you will have to reclaim the feelings that you denied in order to help you survive childhood. People *cannot* recover from co-dependency without reclaiming their feelings.

Healing Your Inner Child. If you grew up in a dysfunctional family, you were taught to focus on what others were doing and not on what you were doing. You were forced to adopt a false self in order to please others. You also were forced to hide your true self, including your innocent, vulnerable inner child. Your inner child suffered from wounds administered by supposedly caring, loving people who may have laughed at you, teased you, showed no respect for you, not listened to you, physically beat you or ignored your most important needs. To keep from getting hurt, it may have been necessary for you to hide that part of you from the outside world. In the process, you also may have hidden that part from yourself. Recovery involves reconnecting with and healing your inner child.

Defining Your Own Boundaries. Everyone has a psychological territory that is their own. It consists of your thoughts, feelings, behaviors and your body. Most people who came from a dysfunctional family had their territory violated so often as a child that as an adult they no longer are even aware of when it is happening. Most co-dependents have a very low awareness of their personal boundaries and almost no skills in defining and protecting their boundaries. It is essential for co-dependents to learn to define and protect their boundaries in effective ways if they wish to break their co-dependent patterns.

Learning To Be Intimate. Co-dependents both fear and desire intimacy. The fear is often that they will be controlled, hurt, engulfed or trampled by someone with whom they are intimate. Breaking co-dependency seems to require a rebonding process with another human being. People often need new parenting from someone like a therapist or another adult who can supply the missing information, touch or the nurturing support necessary to build object constancy and self-esteem.

Learning New Forms of Relationship. Most people who have lived with co-dependent patterns for some time have little or no awareness of the richness of life that they are missing. Often it is some vague awareness that "There has to be more to life than this" that allows co-dependent people to start taking the risks to change. What replaces co-dependency is interdependency, where two or more people have learned to be autonomous enough to be able to co-create life together and to be willing to support the highest good in each other.

Case Example

Bill and Sara had been married for about eight years when trouble began. Sara was the first to feel the need to change. She was a people–pleaser all her life and did an excellent job of taking care of Bill's needs. In fact, her total worth as a person was dependent on taking care of Bill. She had come from an alcoholic family and watched both her mother and father die of alcohol-related illnesses. She was raised by an aunt and uncle who also drank heavily. Bill was naturally very surprised when Sara announced to him one day how unhappy she was, because he had thought he was the only one who was unhappy. There were lots of fights and Bill felt controlled by Sara's caretaking. His mother had used a similar way to control him and invade his space. Bill felt that he could not do anything successfully on his own. His mother always seemed to undermine his self-esteem by taking over when he made a mistake. He had started his own business several years ago and he kept the financial end of the business secret from Sara, fearing that she might criticize his handling of the business. The business was not allowing Bill to fully support himself so Sara supported both of them on her salary. With Bill withholding information on the business, Sara became even more distrusting of Bill.

Things came to a head when Sara announced that she could not have sex with Bill anymore. She had lost her sexual feelings early in the marriage but continued to have sex with Bill because she thought that was what a good wife should do. They had tried couples therapy briefly but Bill was threatened by the therapist. Sara also tried group therapy for co-dependents but found it mostly educational. Both had read the popular literature and had tried to sort out what was going wrong.

Sara came to see me (Barry) the first time because she said she wanted a male therapist to help her better understand men. She readily admitted that she was very co-dependent but needed to know how to break it. I took a cognitive approach with her at first, explaining to Sara the causes of her co-dependency and showing her where she got stuck. She had decided to separate from Bill to sort out the problems. I suggested that the best way to work on breaking co-dependency would be with couples therapy, if Bill would be willing to come with her for three sessions to see if it might work. She agreed to ask him.

The next session, both of them showed up to work with both of us. Bill was scared and resistant at first. However, by the end of the session he began to see how therapy could help. Both of them committed themselves to working together to break their co-dependency. Sara had complained about Bill's intrusion into her space, so we helped Sara set boundaries and negotiate an agreement from Bill that he would not come to visit her without calling first. She could decide whether or not she wanted to see him. This was the first actual personal boundary she had ever set in their relationship, and we both impressed on Bill the importance of his keeping the agreement in order to begin to build trust.

As homework, Sara agreed to begin to write a list of her wants and needs for Bill and to come prepared to practice asking for what she wanted or needed from him at our next session. She also agreed to go talk to her aunt and uncle and get as much information as she could about her mother, who died when Sara was ten, and about her father, who died when she was seventeen.

As Sara and Bill entered our office for their next session, we could see something had changed. Sara was animated and jovial, while Bill seemed much more relaxed. Sara quickly announced that she had experienced some major breakthroughs. She had recently visited her aunt and uncle. While she was asking them questions about her childhood, her uncle blew up and pounded his fist on the table. She had started to cry, and suddenly all the sadness and anger she had been holding in for so long came pouring out. She was able to tell her aunt and uncle what it was really like for her growing up and, though they were shocked, they listened intently as she poured out her feelings.

That night she went home and, for the first time, wrote out a long list of things that she wanted or needed from Bill. She was prepared to ask Bill for them in a clear way, knowing she deserved them. She reported renewed energy and lots of insights. Bill also had some breakthroughs of his own and, for the first time, he saw how controlling and invasive his mother had been and how he had projected that onto Sara. He announced that he was going to have his brother, a banker, put his books in order and then share them completely with Sara so she could begin to cooperate with him in his business. They also announced that they were going to take a class in co-dependency offered through a local church so they could work together more in breaking their co-dependent patterns.

Bill expressed his fear of losing Sara. He asked her how long it was going to take her until she would have sex with him again. She looked right at him in a loving way and said, "As long as it takes me to clear away my blocks so I will *want* to have sex with you again. I won't do it out of guilt or obligation anymore. The more you cooperate and the more I find out that I can trust you to keep your agreements, the shorter the time it will take. I love you and I want to work this out with you." Bill breathed a sigh of relief and agreed to work with her to do his part in building trust.

It seemed appropriate at that point in the session to talk to them about surrender. I (Barry) said, "The core issue for both of you is surrender, which has a masculine and a feminine form. Bill, you need Sara to help you develop the feminine form, which is the willingness to receive without resistance. This will be very difficult, particularly when you put your mother's face on Sara. Sara, your issue is learning the masculine form, which is the willingness to take charge of yourself without guilt. Bill may be able to help you with this one as well." Sara quickly announced, "You know I haven't felt guilty since I talked to my aunt and uncle. I feel free from it now and I hope it doesn't come back."

Sara and Bill have a good chance of breaking out of the co-dependency trap if they continue to work together like this. They are in a committed relationship where they can do most of the healing they need to do. They have couples therapy to help them learn the skills and tools they need. They have a class to attend together where they can discuss their relationship. Finally, they both are developing tools through therapy and their reading so they can work on themselves alone. The time they are living apart could be a valuable time for them to develop their independence and begin to find effective ways to work on their own issues without the help of any other person. This will help them become stronger individuals with more object constancy and higher self-esteem. This individual strength will help them weather the stormy seas ahead as they find ways to work together to break their co-dependency.

Summary

If individuals in a relationship have not reached this stage of cooperation and commitment, it can take much longer to achieve major breakthroughs. Even with breakthroughs, such as the ones described above, there is much hard work involved in the process of breaking co-dependent relationship patterns. Our estimate is that even when you have a committed, cooperative relationship where both of you are working on breaking free of the co-dependency trap, it can still take anywhere from two to five years of work to get beyond your major co-dependent patterns.

CHAPTER SEVEN

Facing Your Problem

As with any dysfunctional pattern of behavior, the severity of the symptoms of co-dependency may be located on a continuum that ranges from very subtle to glaringly obvious. In co-dependent relationships that are basically harmonious, the symptoms can be very subtle—simple things such as who drives, who speaks first, who manages the money and how parenting responsibilities are shared. Such behaviors, symptoms of the rigid cultural roles of a dominator system, are more difficult to identify because they are so unconscious. Recognizing and changing these behaviors requires that you examine closely your daily routine of actions and responses to your partner. Reversing roles for a while on a specific behavior pattern is a useful way to create both awareness and a new pattern. After a period of reversing roles, you may then want to negotiate around the behavior when it arises. ("Will you drive today?")

In relationships involving psychological abuse, the symptoms are more obvious. In relationships involving physical abuse, the symptoms are very obvious. People involved in abusive relationships are often long-term victims. They may suffer years of neglect, poverty, humiliation, incest or rape in a relationship that survives because the victim fears abandonment or fears for his or her life. In such instances, denial is a primary way by which victims prevent themselves from experiencing their pain and suffering.

THE ROOTS OF DENIAL

Denial is a defense mechanism used to help avoid things that are unpleasant. The unpleasant things you are avoiding may be your feelings, a belief or the fear of loss or abandonment. Denial enables you to avoid seeing what is really going on and to avoid feeling what is going on inside you. Denial is an especially useful tool for small children who find themselves in the midst of chaos or violence, drunkenness, abuse, neglect and abandonment. Denial can make the pain and fear go away. The main purpose of denial is self-protection and survival.

Most people learn about denial from their parents, who learned about it from *their* parents. Most families have silent, unwritten rules that prohibit such things as open expression of feelings, direct and honest communication, being open and vulnerable, showing imperfections, being selfish, playing and having fun, discussing problems openly, doing things that cause change in the family and, especially, being an autonomous person. These rules are frequently summarized by such all-encompassing dictums as "don't talk", "don't think", "don't feel" and "don't trust."

In dysfunctional families, these kinds of rules serve the purpose of avoiding or denying conflict. If the truth were spoken and acknowledged, confrontations would be inevitable. That might cause explosive changes in the family system. As a result, denial is often the only response many families have to a problem, since members often have neither the awareness to see the problem nor the skills to work it through. Members are taught that peace and equilibrium must be maintained at all costs, even if members have to develop a false self.

You may have created a false self because you perceived that who you really are was not acceptable to the adults around you. When, as a child, you innocently spoke some truth and you found yourself being punished, you soon learned to be quiet or to speak what was expected. Through trial and error you discovered the unspoken rules about what was permissible and what was expected. You learned to discount the spoken messages and base your behavior on what you experienced.

Discounting

Discounting is one way that parents and families reinforce children and other adults in denying their internal world. Discounting means not paying attention to your own needs, wants, feelings, ideas or abilities. It means undervaluing or overvaluing yourself or others. It can also involve forgetting or ignoring important facts or information. Ultimately, it involves discounting yourself, discounting others and discounting the situation.

"Counting" is the opposite of discounting. It supports the needs, wants, feelings, ideas and abilities of yourself, others and the situation. It allows you to be responsible for how you respond to people and situations. This means that you recognize that other people don't "make" you feel a certain way, that you can determine how you feel in response to what others do.

Here are some common forms of discounting and counting:

	Discounting	*Counting*
Others	• Interrupting • Sarcasm • Not looking at someone who is speaking to you • Not giving reasons for actions	• Listening • Talking straight • Looking directly at people • Saying, "This is why I did X."

	Discounting	Counting
Self	• Accepting what others say without questioning • Losing or breaking things and "trashing out" property	• Asking "What do I think about it?" • Valuing, appreciating and being responsible for property
Situation	• Forgetting to do things • Giving up • Believing the problem will go away	• Keeping agreements • Looking for solutions • Looking at the facts

"For Your Own Good"

Having to repress your feelings, thoughts and dreams about yourself, and the fragile parts of the person you really were, is an unconscious form of cruelty imposed by your well-meaning parents during your early childhood. Many of the messages and forms of discipline that taught you to deny your real self were given to you by parents and other authority figures who believed they were doing it "for your own good." As a child it was probably hard to believe that you needed harsh punishment, criticism, humiliation, shame, ridicule and neglect. Because you regarded your parents and teachers as intelligent, all-knowing protectors, you accepted their judgment and believed them when they told you it was all good for you and that you must really deserve it.

This form of child-rearing, which supports the denial mechanism in families, comes from what is known as "the vicious cycle of cruelty." (Weinhold 1988) This phenomenon is a pattern in which the devastating effects of cruelty are passed on from one person to another person in order to get revenge for the cruelty done to them. Examples of this are bullying and child abuse. Children who were bullied or abused almost always grow up to be bullies or abusers of others. Passing on the cruelty to someone else is an attempt to relieve the feelings of anger and rage that they were unable to express when they were being treated cruelly. Adolf Hitler is an example of an abused child who carried out the vicious cycle of cruelty to an extreme degree. His father beat and abused him while also indoctrinating him about the evilness of the Jews. This helped set the stage for his hatred of Jews and his need for revenge as an adult. (Miller 1983)

It is important for you to recognize the "for your own good" incidents in your childhood as forms of vicious cruelty done to you by well-meaning people who were acting out unconscious urges and who were given false information. It is also important to remember that your parents did the best they could with what skills and awarenesses they had and that the vicious cycle of cruelty is a very unconscious process. This is illustrated by the oath that many people make as a child that they will never treat their children the way they were treated. Yet, in disciplining their own children, they are often shocked to find themselves using the same kinds of punishment and frequently even the same words that were used to punish them as a child.

Dishonesty: A Form of Denial

The vicious cycle of cruelty is also used to enforce other forms of dysfunctional behavior, such as dishonesty. A lack of honesty in parent-child interactions undermines the child's ability to trust both himself or herself and others. This creates a feeling of distrust about the child's inner world of self-experience and about their external world of expectations and false messages. Eventually the child's world becomes split in two and he or she has to choose between the two worlds. Because the external world has more power and authority and because of the child's strong need for bonding and affection, the child will almost always choose the external world. At this point, the child must do something with the feelings and experience of his or her internal world. Shutting them out by denying them is a common reaction. They find that this decision is supported by their parents, family and friends who also made the same choice as children.

This allows the child to detach from himself/herself in the midst of crisis. Typical denial responses might be:

- to minimize the situation ("It's no big deal.")

- to pretend something isn't happening ("No, this can't be happening.")

- to repress their feelings ("I don't really care.")

- to avoid their feelings (sleeping, obsessing, working more or using other compulsive behaviors)

- to numb themselves (drugs, alcohol, food or other addictive substances).

Denial and Craziness

Denial is actually a form of self-dishonesty. Separating yourself from your feelings and pretending to feel something that you are not is lying to yourself. In learning to lie to yourself you are setting the stage for deceiving others. In a family where all members have been trained in self-deception, there will be wholesale lying. The result is dishonest relationships.

Nothing can make you feel "crazy" quicker than being lied to. Each of us has a deep part of ourself that recognizes truth. When our brain is given information that does not match our inner truth or experience, we suffer from a "shorted circuit" that literally makes us feel crazy. In such instances it requires a great deal of self-confidence to trust our internal knowing more than the information given us by authority figures. Most children do not have a sufficient reservoir of self-confidence to counter the external information. As a result, most children experience life as chaotic and crazy.

The Happy Family Syndrome

Dishonest people eventually must lie to the world in order to maintain the lying within the family system. In families where there is alcoholism, sexual abuse or violence, there are rigid rules about not telling what really goes on at home. Members are frequently threatened with further abuse or violence if they tell the family secrets. Family members put up a good front even though chaos exists at home. They learn to live a lie that further extends their crazy-making experiences. In this "living-a-lie" form of "The Happy Family Syndrome," the participants are somewhat aware of the discrepancy between what really happens and what they pretend happens. What holds this form together is a conspiracy against telling the truth. In the larger community, these same families may be perceived as stable and upstanding.

A second form of The Happy Family Syndrome is "living a fantasy." This form usually afflicts an individual and may or may not affect others in the family system. Individuals affected with this fantasy are extremely difficult to treat in therapy. They may seek help because of some life crisis, like a divorce or a job loss. Typically these people will recall their childhood as one that was almost idyllic. They describe the family and their experiences of childhood in such glowing terms that it begins to sound like "Leave It To Beaver" or "Father Knows Best." Such descriptions indicate that the person has created a "fantasy world" memory to support their needs and to deny their feelings and internal experiences.

Denial in Relationships

Children who are not provided with adequate bonding or who are abandoned, abused or neglected move through life looking for people who can provide nurturing, security and affection. Their need for these missing things makes them dream that some kindly person, perhaps a kind maiden or a dashing knight, will appear in their life. When some person eventually does appear, these expected qualities will be "projected" onto the person whether they are capable of living them or not. This phenomenon, also known as infatuation or idealization, serves a valuable psychological function for the dreamer who believes his/her long-unfulfilled needs are finally going to be met. The dreaming phenomenon also keeps the dreamer from having to feel the old feelings related to being poorly bonded, abandoned, abused or neglected. The dreaming or idealizing may go on for many years in spite of information and experiences that totally refute the person's dream.

An example of this kind of dreaming is the woman who needs a warm and affectionate husband. During their courtship her husband is attentive and caring and she experiences her dreams coming true. She continues to dream he is warm and attentive even after he turns alcoholic and becomes abusive. Her dreams support her through the rough times when he stays out all night, comes home drunk or hits her. She is able to make excuses that explain his "uncharacteristic" behavior so that her "dream come true" can continue.

The difficulty with this dreaming and denial in relationships is that it keeps the dreamer from really getting his or her needs met and it creates a new reservoir of unexpressed feelings. It can also support dysfunctional behavioral patterns in both individuals and families, sometimes to the point of contributing to life-threatening situations such as battering. In these kinds of situations, the person may continue to dream positive qualities onto the partner until a crisis finally may break the dream sufficiently so that the dreamer finally takes in the real information.

Breaking Through Denial

It is important to remember that denial in its various forms is a cultural pattern that has been handed down from generation to generation and that it is passed on by well-meaning parents and other adults who have not been aware. If you have found yourself participating in this process, do not beat on yourself. You also have been doing the best you could, and you will be able to do better now that you know there is a better way.

In order to break the pattern of denial, there are several important tasks that must be completed. All of them are designed to help you find your real self—your real feelings, needs, wants, ideas, thoughts and dreams. These tasks include:

- learning to recognize and refute discounts
- learning to give "counts"

- listening reflectively
- asking for and receiving feedback on how others see you
- discovering holes in your awareness
- accepting your inner world of experience as valuable
- recognizing the "dream" or vision you have for your relationship and checking it with reality
- asking your partner what his or her dream or vision is for your relationship and checking it against yours
- finding out if you are addicted to a person, substance or activity by seeing if you can live without it for five straight days without major discomfort.

TOOLS FOR BREAKING THROUGH DENIAL

Tools for Working Alone

- *Keep a journal that you use at least daily.* Write down what you have experienced in your interactions with people during the day. Record your feelings, reactions and dreams.

- *Learn to recognize a signal in your body that tells you when you hear dishonesty.* It may come as a tightening of a muscle, as a knot in your stomach or a pain in your head. When this signal comes, be ready to acknowledge it and spend some time reflecting on the situation to discover the area of untruth.

Tools for Therapy

- *Use a reality approach that examines the information available from your past to create a picture of what really happened to you as a child.* Gather information about past and present relationships to bring into therapy to use in creating the picture.

- *Learn about "sequencing" or breaking down old, dysfunctional patterns of behavior into steps.* Look at each step to see where there is a hole in your awareness about what happens during the replay of the pattern. Use sequencing to find out where the pattern or behavior takes a dysfunctional turn. This is the place where you, your partner or both of you will need a change in behavior.

Tools for Support Groups

- *Make contracts with fellow group members.* Ask them to give you feedback when you discount.

- *Learn to recognize when you rescue or persecute and to recognize when it is being done to you.* Watch group dynamics and discuss your perceptions with group members.

- *Learn to recognize your own need to be a victim.* Ask group members to help you. When you complain a lot, request they stop you by asking, "What do you want?" Learn to do this for others who play victim.

Tools for Partnerships

- *Create a "No Discount Contract" with your partner.* Make an agreement not to discount each other. In your contract you will both agree, for a specific length of time (several weeks or a month), to avoid discounting. You will also need to determine what consequences you each want if you forget. Your contract might stipulate things such as the following:

    1. When you say what you don't like, say it in a way that I don't feel "put down."

    2. "If I discount you, I want you to remind me by _____
       _____."

    3. "This contract is in effect for _____ week(s)/month(s). At that time we will decide if we want to renegotiate and/or continue it."

- *Create a common vision for your relationship.* Set aside a day with your partner where you will not be interrupted. Take a trip, send the children out with a babysitter, unplug the phone or take a picnic to a quiet spot. Working individually at first, write down your dream for yourself—what you'd like to do personally and professionally in the next year. Then share your individual dream with your partner. Look for areas of mutual interest and then create a shared dream or vision.

- *Develop reflective listening skills.* During conversations with your partner, stop periodically to summarize what you have heard him or her say. For example, "What I'm hearing you say is. . . ."

- *Create a ritual or activity that recognizes the end of the old form of relationship that you've had.* Such activities might include a burial in which you fill a small box with reminders of the past and bury it. You could also place the reminders or slips of papers that describe the old patterns on a funeral pyre and burn them. Another possibility is to find small rocks or stones that represent the old ideas or ways of behavior and throw them into a creek or pond one at a time. As you throw each rock, say, "I release ＿＿＿＿＿＿ (old pattern) as a way of being together with ＿＿＿＿＿＿ (partner's name)." Such activities actually help our brain release the dysfunctional patterns we have stored there.

Case Example

Sandra and Russ came to us for divorce counseling just weeks before their divorce was to be final. They had been married seventeen years and had four children. They had been active in the Catholic Church since childhood and centered many of their family activities around parish events. For nearly ten years, they had led marriage enrichment weekends for other couples and had what seemed to be an ideal family life.

Sandra worked part-time to supplement the family income

so that they could send the children to parochial schools. She was active in scouting and catechism class and saw her professional role as mother and wife. When she described her life with Russ and the children, her story was filled with happiness and contentment. Russ had been a supportive partner who, until recently, had been the perfect husband and father. They had experienced a few rough spots, but she had been shocked when he suddenly announced that he wanted a divorce and was moving out.

Russ, who owned a small business, sat slumped in silence as Sandra told her story of their relationship. Obviously depressed, he began to tell his side. From the very beginning, he had felt misgivings about trying to create the happy family dream that Sandra had. Even as a child he had felt rebellious and resentful at the strict rules of Catholicism. He never wanted four children and had come to resent the financial burden that private schooling for them had become. He confessed that he felt lost and exhausted. He had tried his best to do all the things that were supposed to make people happy and it hadn't worked. Russ explained how he had tried so hard to fulfill his part of the happy family dream. He was at the point where he felt he would die if he didn't get out of the trap soon.

In talking further with Russ and Sandra, it was clear they came to counseling with very different dreams. Sandra wished that the session would end in a reconciliation so that the happy family dream could return. Russ, on the other hand, was quite clear he had come for divorce counseling. He wanted support in making Sandra see how desperate he was to get out of the dream that was killing him.

Further inquiry into the couple's history revealed that Russ had periodically tried to tell Sandra that the relationship wasn't working for him. Each time this had happened, however, Sandra had managed to persuade him that it was working, either by discounting, making him feel guilty or persuading him that the realization of the dream was right around the corner.

Denial in this relationship was rampant. Russ continually denied the severity of his own experience until he finally felt his death was imminent. Sandra repeatedly denied information from Russ when he said it wasn't working. She denied both the verbal and the non-verbal information he gave her. She was able to avoid seeing Russ's slumped, defeated posture, his increasing thinness, his sunken eyes and obvious depression. Sandra's need for her own happy family dream to come true was so strong that she was still dreaming, in this session, that it would happen.

Russ was very firm about his plan to continue with the divorce and to maintain his separate living quarters. He indicated that he had little to give toward parenting and really needed time alone to think and nurture himself.

We saw clearly Russ's determination to end the relationship and believed his statement that he felt as if he were dying. As therapists, our task seemed to be to help Sandra through her denial by making sure she fully received and accepted Russ's information and feedback.

When Sandra saw that the session was indeed divorce counseling and not marriage counseling, her armor of hope shattered. She began to weep softly as we asked Russ to repeat his feelings to her until she really took them in.

The final part of the session focused on helping Sandra accept Russ's decision and also to see how her perception of the last years of their marriage had really been a dream. This was very difficult for her to do. Each time the reality of divorce and the end of her dream penetrated her, she broke into sobs of despair. We quietly supported her feelings of grief and sat with them both until they seemed to have reached a mutual reality. They looked briefly at each other, got up to leave and then it was over—the denial of feelings, the denial of the unhappiness in the relationship and the old form of relationship.

Summary

Denial is one of the most difficult human conditions to deal with. The more old pain and feelings we have "stuffed," the more difficult denial is to break through. It is important to look truthfully at our past and our parents to realize that everyone did the best they knew how. That way, we don't get stuck in blaming. It is also important to develop skills in conflict resolution so that we can work through the conflicts that emerge from telling the truth and breaking the "happy family" illusion. With good tools and skills, these conflicts can become doorways to creating real intimacy in a family.

CHAPTER EIGHT

Understanding the Causes of Co-dependency

To find the causes of co-dependent patterns in your adult relationships, you will have to look back in time to your early childhood where the roots of the problem exist. Most people don't remember what happened to them in early childhood. You may remember a few selected events but chances are that, if you compared notes with others who were actually present at these events, they would remember them quite differently. Several important facts about human behavior make the task of remembering more workable:

- It isn't important that you remember actual events; what you have acted upon may be not what actually happened, but your belief or *perception* of what actually happened.

- It is important to remember the feelings that go with your perceptions. Your feelings are a more accurate record and are stored in your body as memories.

- All the information you seek about your past usually is available in your present behavior and your present relationships. Your present relationships are a replay of the unresolved issues from your earlier relationships.

- Therefore, all the causes of co-dependency stemming from unresolved co-dependencies in early childhood will show up in your current relationships and will press for resolution and completion.

This becomes easier to see if you begin to look at your current co-dependent patterns this way. When people "fall in love," there is a kind of falling back in time. Scott Peck (1978:88) describes it this way: "In some respects (but certainly not in all) the act of falling in love is an act of regression. The experience of merging with the loved one has its echoes from the time when we were merged with our mothers in infancy."

The following examples illustrate this phenomenon. As an infant you nursed at your mother's breast or were held and given a bottle. For you at that age there was no time; it was only the blissful present that you could comprehend.

Compare this with the words of a client who at the time she said these words was describing her co-dependent relationship: "We don't see each other very often and I begin to yearn for closeness with him. Then we get together and time seems to stand still. When we make love I forget about his drinking and all the times he yelled at me. I want the good feeling between us to last forever. But it doesn't and he starts drinking again."

When you wanted to be fed as an infant, you cried, but sometimes your mother couldn't respond immediately. To you this must have seemed like an eternity even though it may have been only a few minutes.

Now listen to another client's words and notice the similarity:

I called Melody on the phone and there was no answer. I knew she sometimes did some shopping after work and didn't get home right away, but I felt anxious, like she was unavailable for me. At first I thought, 'I'll call her in about an hour,' but five minutes later I called again and kept calling every five minutes for the next hour. I was frantic. All kinds of thoughts went through my head. Was she angry at me? Was she out with someone else? Was she in an accident? I couldn't let go of these thoughts . . .''

The roots of co-dependency are easy to understand. You started out as a helpless infant who could not survive without the care of your parents. Nature created a symbiotic relationship with them that provided you with at least three main things:

- It kept you alive and cared for.

- It gave you the illusion that you would always be safe and cared for.

- It gave you the illusion that you were very powerful.

Understandably, you held on to this as long as possible despite a competing desire to become a separate person and despite your parents' attempts to wean you from this co-dependency.

In almost every case, a parent is not able to be perfectly tuned in to the child. Therefore, some of your needs to spend more time in this blissful state were probably not met. Your parents had other things to do and had their own needs, worries and problems. They may have gotten depressed or physically ill or had certain beliefs about child-rearing that frustrated your need for oneness. They may have believed in schedule feeding or believed that responding to your needs too often would spoil you. Whatever happened to interfere with the process of getting these needs met, it is likely you still have some unmet needs for the timeless bliss you dimly remember.

These are normal needs of adults that can be met in a close relationship. What complicates the process, however, is the belief that you have to recreate a co-dependent relationship in order to get these needs met. If you never learned the necessary skills to become psychologically separate and autonomous, your only choice seems to be to recreate a relationship similar to the original symbiotic relationship you had with your parents. Many parents don't know how to teach their children to be separate, while others, because of their own needs to hold on to their children, undermine the efforts of their children to become separate.

People who didn't become "separate" often feel a more desperate need for a return to this blissful state of oneness. You will hear them say:

- "I don't feel alive unless I am in a love relationship with a (man or woman)."

- "I don't feel complete as a person without him/her. She/he makes me feel like a whole person."

- I would die if I ever lost her/him. My life wouldn't be worth living. I could never be happy again."

- "When I'm not with him/her I feel very insecure. When we cuddle up together, I feel really safe."

Co-dependency grows out of the illusion that your mother or father, on whom you counted to make you feel good or safe or secure, *now* exists in the person with whom you have a relationship. Our whole culture, especially popular music, films and television programs, reinforces this illusion. Your main goals in life become:

- to find any way possible to hold on to that person and make them love you the way you remember once being loved or cared for by your mother or father or

- to help you complete your unfinished business with your mother or father.

Of course this never works over the long haul and it leads to manipulation and control rather than to enduring love. What is missing in this plan is a full awareness of the sources of the problem and tools for understanding how to correct the problem. Unfortunately most people don't see these problems until they are already enmeshed in a co-dependent relationship or after they have gone through numerous relationships with similar results.

Frequently the most dysfunctional co-dependent behaviors don't show up until a couple is close enough to provide the safety necessary for these patterns to surface. Couples can live together for years and not experience these dysfunctional patterns. Then they get married. The commitment of the marriage contract often creates enough safety to allow the patterns to surface. Also, a marriage relationship can bring comparisons with the couple's birth families to the surface for the first time. Add to this the cultural illusions about relationships that are supported by the mass media, and you can see why many of the illusions that create co-dependency persist so long.

TOOLS FOR UNDERSTANDING THE CAUSES OF CO-DEPENDENCY

The book *Playing Grown-up Is Serious Business: Breaking Free of Addictive Family Patterns* (Weinhold 1988) is an excellent tool for understanding the causes of co-dependency. The book presents information on the twelve different patterns of dysfunctional behavior that are learned during childhood and are recycled in adult relationships. A major portion of the book contains self-awareness activities to help people identify the patterns. In addition, the second half of the book offers useful suggestions on how to break those patterns.

Tools for Working Alone

- *Take a look at your anger and resentments.* Make two lists. On one list write: "I resent my mother for . . ." and on the second list write: "I resent my father for . . ." After you have completed those two lists, you may have a clearer idea of the issues you are dealing with. Then write a third list headed by: "I resent my partner for . . ." You will likely begin to see that many of your current resentments have their roots in childhood and represent unresolved conflicts from childhood. Another list may be headed with: "I resent myself for . . ." You may be blaming yourself for many of the same things for which you blame others.

• *Make a list of the things you remember your mother or father disapproving of in you and others when you were a child.* Then place a check mark (√) next to those things you disapprove of in yourself and an (x) next to those things you disapprove of in others. What frequently happens is that we inadvertently take on the beliefs, values, prejudices and fears of our parents. Are you still very sensitive to the kind of disapproval you get from your partner that resembles in some way the disapproval of your parents? These represent unhealed wounds from childhood that can be healed with the help of your partner. Chapter Seventeen contains more information on how to heal these in committed relationships.

Tools for Therapy

Therapy can be a good place to examine in depth what actually happened to you as a child. You may have created a "happy childhood fantasy" for yourself to help you avoid the awful reality of it. A therapist who understands the dynamics of co-dependency can help you correct any distorted views of your childhood you might hold and then help you create a more accurate picture of it.

A therapist can also help you to see what decisions you may have made about yourself when you were a child and whether or not those decisions ("I can't do anything right", "I'm ugly", "I'm no good.") still rule your life and your relationships. Because many people have poor self-esteem or weak object constancy, they have trouble maintaining a positive self-image in the face of criticism or perceived mistakes. A good therapist can really help you build your self-esteem, strengthen your object constancy and help you design "homework" activities to help you learn to be successful.

Tools for Support Groups

- *In the groups you attend, notice who reminds you of your father and mother.* Identify what characteristics you seem to have trouble dealing with in others and trace those back to one of your parents. Notice how you react to these people. This will tell you how you must have reacted to your parents, in case you have forgotten.

- *Ask group members to role play conflict situations with you.* Try acting out situations you had with one of your parents and learn to make new, more effective responses to this parent. Ask other group members to help coach you in making better responses.

Tools for Partnerships

- *Separately, you and your partner each make a list of traits that describe your mother and your father.* The list can be constructed as you see them now or as you remember them from childhood. If there were other significant adults who helped to raise you, like a grandparent or even an older sibling, make a list of their characteristics as well. You should be able to list at least ten traits for each person.

  After you have finished writing your list, do the following things:

  1. Place a check (√) mark next to those traits that you see in yourself.

  2. Place a plus (+) sign next to the positive traits you chose and a minus (−) sign next to the negative traits you chose.

  3. Place an (x) next to those traits you see in your relationship partner(s), such as husband, wife, lover, close friends.

  4. Discuss together the patterns that emerge from the lists. Ask yourself the following questions and compare your answers:

- With which parent do I most identify? Which parent do I see most in my partner?
- Do I see more of the positive or negative traits of my parent(s) in myself? My partner?
- Who did I have the most conflict with while growing up, mother or father? How do the traits I chose relate to that conflict? Do I have similar conflicts with my partner?

This exercise can generate a good discussion between you and your partner regarding the unfinished business you may be trying to finish in your current relationship. Remember the law of human development: anything left unresolved or incomplete in your life will persist and press for completion. If you and your partner can begin to see that the causes of your current conflicts are rooted in both of your past histories, then you may begin to understand what is trying to get completed in your current relationship. Without that kind of awareness, it is almost impossible to break out of the co-dependency trap. Couples will continue to recycle these unresolved issues over and over again and not get through them.

Case Example

Dora and Melvin were married thirty-seven years when they first came to therapy with us. Dora was very unhappy with Melvin and their relationship. Melvin seemed to be unaware of these problems and came to therapy at Dora's insistence. In the initial therapy sessions, their separate descriptions of their relationship painted far different pictures, each blaming the other for their problems. What became apparent was that both of them had a high investment in being "right" and making the other one "wrong." The first couple of sessions were like a battleground. It looked as if we weren't going to be able to help them to resolve their problems. Each of them took a turn blaming the other and then collapsing into helplessness and hopelessness.

What we decided to do was support their helplessness and hopelessness. We started saying things like, "This sure looks to us like a hopeless situation. We have never seen a relationship that was so hopeless." This was a risk because they could have taken our words as permission to leave the relationship. However, we didn't think that would happen because (1) they had been married for thirty-seven years, which indicated some staying power and (2) they were very co-dependent and probably could survive a dysfunctional relationship better than doing without that relationship.

The strategy began to work. However, it wasn't until we also asked them to recall other times in their life when they felt helpless and hopeless that the crucial information began to surface. Dora said she remembered feeling helpless and hopeless many times as a child. She admitted that she still feels that way in her relationship with her father. She described him as judgmental and a perfectionist. She said that no matter what she did, he would find something wrong with it. While growing up, she felt she was never right and she felt emotionally abandoned by him. She desperately wanted his approval and praise for her accomplishments, but it never came. She would try very hard to please him only to have him be critical of her efforts.

Dora's story seemed to help Melvin remember some similar things. He said, "My mother was a lot like that. I tried everything I could to please her and it never worked. Finally when I was eighteen she had to go to a mental institution." With tears in his eyes, Melvin continued, "I tried to help her but she still went away. I felt as if it was my fault that she went crazy. I just didn't know what to do to make her feel better. Everything I tried was the wrong thing."

Now we knew why it was so important for them to be right. All their lives they had this deep-seated fear of being wrong. Each had a strong unfulfilled need to be seen as right by their partner. One of the first things we did with Dora and Melvin was to have them ask for positive feedback from each other. They needed to know that it was possible to be right in the eyes of their partner. Their first efforts at this process were clumsy, and it was hard for each of them to take in the compliments and kind words. Initially, they discounted what was being said in subtle ways, such as body twitches and by slightly turning away from each other. With our help, they continued until they started absorbing the positive feedback.

The next step was to get them to become more functionally autonomous with each other in their relationship. One area where they were very co-dependent was in doing household chores. Dora had a list of things she wanted Melvin to do around the house. Because he was retired and she still had her business in her home, she was always busy. Melvin, however, wanted to relax and watch television and putter around the house. In order to please Dora, Melvin would agree to do the things she had on her list. Then he would become afraid that he would do them in the wrong order or not be able to do them to her satisfaction. Filled with the fear of being criticized for doing the wrong thing, he would then withdraw and watch television or take naps. When Melvin did this, Dora experienced abandonment just like she did from her father. Dora would nag Melvin about the unfinished items on the list. When she did that, Dora would remind him of his critical, controlling mother. He would then withdraw even more until a major conflict erupted between them. The intensity of the conflict helped restore contact.

We were able to get Dora and Melvin to agree to prepare separate job lists. Dora agreed that either she would do the things Melvin wasn't willing to do or they would pay someone else to do them. Melvin also felt left out when Dora worked long hours, so he began to ask her to do more fun things with him. In addition, Melvin began to do more things on his own without Dora's nagging. They began to cooperate with each other more on day-to-day activities and developed a feeling of good will, and some mutuality began to develop between them. During the first year, they would return to therapy when they would get stuck, but, as of now, they have been functioning well without the support of therapy for almost a year.

Summary

When couples begin to understand the causes of their co-dependent patterns and are given some specific tools for working on these patterns on their own, they no longer need therapy and can extend the healing to themselves. It is easy to see that in the case described above, Dora and Melvin could have continued indefinitely in their co-dependent patterns, making themselves and each other very miserable. When couples begin to understand the causes of their problems and can stop blaming each other, they can move closer together and deepen their relationships. They can let go of the need to control each other and find effective, cooperative ways to get their needs and wants met.

CHAPTER NINE

Unraveling Co-dependent Relationships

IDENTIFYING CO-DEPENDENT PATTERNS

The next step in the recovery process is learning to identify the co-dependent patterns as they exist in your current relationships. Co-dependency is so common that it is sometimes difficult to sort out co-dependent relationship patterns from the more functional patterns of relationship.

The following are some of the *key* indicators of a co-dependent relationship:

- Even though you have lots of objective evidence that the relationship as it stands is not good for you, you take no steps to change it or break the co-dependent patterns.

- You find yourself making excuses for you or your partner that are designed to hide the truth from others.

- When you think about changing or leaving the relationship, you feel afraid and cling to it even harder.

- When you take some beginning steps to change the relationship, you suffer acute anxiety and physical symptoms that can only be relieved by reestablishing the old co-dependent patterns.

- When you do begin to make changes, you experience an intense longing for the old patterns, or you feel scared, all alone or empty.

The main characteristics of co-dependent people are as follows.

CO-DEPENDENTS:

- Use an external frame of reference. Co-dependents focus all of their attention on what their partner is doing or not doing.

- Use the relationship the way someone might use alcohol or drugs. They are addicted to another person and believe they can't function independently of that person or without the relationship they have with that person.

- Cannot define their psychological boundaries. Co-dependents don't know where they end and others begin. They tend to take on the problems of others as their own.

- Try always to make a good impression on others. This is a way in which co-dependent people try to control the perceptions of others. They are people-pleasers.

- Do not trust their own ideas, perceptions, feelings or beliefs. Co-dependents will defer to the opinions of others and not stand by their own ideas and opinions.

- Try to make themselves indispensable to others. Co-dependents will knock themselves out to take care of things for others that these people could actually do for themselves.

- Play martyr. They learn to suffer but do it gallantly. They will put up with intolerable situations because they think they have to.

- Are skilled at controlling others. They try to control everything but usually fail because it is an impossible task.

- Are out of touch with their true feelings. They distort their feelings and only express them when they can feel justified to do so.

- Are gullible. Because co-dependents are not in touch with their feelings, they lack discernment. They are bad judges of character and only see what they want to see.

- Lose contact with their spiritual self. They are often cut off from the spiritual side of life.

- Are fearful, rigid and judgmental. Black and white thinking dominates the lives of co-dependents.

Family Roles

In addition to the preceding list of characteristics of co-dependency, there are roles that co-dependents get stuck in which restrict their lives even further. Roles are behaviors that are designed to fill a specific function in a family, usually to keep the co-dependency balanced. Below are the four most common roles that co-dependents play, with indications of the price that must be paid for playing that role.

The Family Hero. These people are often high achievers and act overly responsible. They are the leaders who are football stars or get straight A's. They are often an older child who tends to take life seriously and often doesn't have much fun. Everything is work for them. They become self-disciplined and task-oriented. *The price they pay* is to be tense, rigid and need to be in control to feel comfortable in relationships. They become obsessive and perfectionistic, always concerned about measuring up and being productive. They are usually unable to feel their feelings and tend to separate themselves from others and become isolated and lonely. They usually find co-dependent mates for whom they can take care or be responsible.

The Loner. These people are easy to get along with because they are adept at adjusting and being flexible. They usually don't rock the boat. They avoid leadership positions and stay on the sidelines. They don't get emotionally involved with anything and are careful not to draw attention to themselves. They also may feel a sense of powerlessness. *The price they pay* is to be emotionally blocked and not know how or what they feel. They don't get their needs met, they rarely ask for anything from others directly and they feel isolated and lonely. They are usually depressed and unable to make decisions. They tend to choose co-dependents who cause conflict in their relationship, which keeps them from having to be close.

The Caretaker. These people spend most of their time taking care of other people's emotional needs. They are often warm, sensitive, caring people who know how to listen. They often find themselves taking care of others financially as well. *The price they pay* is that they don't get their own needs met and often feel too guilty to receive anything freely from others. They give to others at their own expense and seek out people who are takers and emotionally needy. They don't experience much intimacy and usually marry someone they can take care of emotionally and/or financially.

The Rebel. These people often act out the dysfunctional patterns of other family members. They get negative attention from parents, teachers and the law. They frequently get their self-esteem needs met by acting against any authority. *The price they pay* is a poor self-image, school failure, being labeled as the "sick one" and the loss of contact with their deep feelings of emotional abandonment covered over by anger. They harbor feelings of resentment and often try to get even with their parents by doing everything the opposite of the way they think their parents would have wanted it. They find mates who will allow them to act out their anger and resentment on them. They are often physically and verbally abusive to their mates, who put up with their behavior.

TOOLS FOR UNRAVELING CO-DEPENDENCY

Tools for Working Alone

The following tool can help bring to the surface some of the unfinished business from your childhood.

- Make two lists. On the first list, write all the things your parents, teachers or other adults did and said to you while you were growing up that you *now* see didn't do you much good and in fact were harmful to you in some way. On the second list, place all the things your parents, teachers or other adults *didn't* say or do to or for you that you *now* realize would have done you some good had they said or done those things.

- After completing the lists, examine them with the following information in mind. The items on the first list represent those things for which you haven't forgiven your parents. These are the things that are holding you back and contributing to your co-dependency. You will need to let go of these things if you intend to break out of the co-dependency trap.

- The second list represents all the things that you are still waiting for someone else to provide for you. You will have to take charge of these things and either ask for them to be met now by your parents or, if that isn't possible, ask other people to help you get these needs met.

- In either case, you will remain stuck in co-dependency until you complete these things. The ultimate in "stuckness" is waiting for someone else to change or provide something for you so you can feel better. You may have a very long wait.

I (Barry) remember doing this exercise with myself and coming up with a long list of things I wish my parents had said to me, such as "I love you just the way you are." On a visit to them some years ago I brought out my list and asked them to tell me, in their own words, all the things I had wanted to hear. They were delighted to do this. I tape-recorded what they said in case I needed reinforcement later. This act helped me let go of some resentment and hurt, and helped me take charge of my own healing process.

Tools for Therapy

One of the most valuable tools you can learn through therapy is to be an objective observer of your own behavior. This enables you to step outside yourself in the midst of a conflict and allows you to observe your behavior. The steps in this process are as follows:

1. Learn to recognize the signals when you are having a co-dependent reaction or flashback. Usually something in the situation rubberbands you back to where the original breakdown in the developmental process occurred. You may find yourself flooded with feelings that are *greater than* the present situation calls for. You may feel anxious, afraid, panicked, outraged, rejected, ashamed, confused or sad. Also you may notice body signals such as increased heart rate, sweating, a pain in your stomach, tightness in your chest or a light-headedness.

2. Take several deep breaths and calm down first before you react any further. Ask yourself, "Am I in any danger in this situation?" If you feel like there is some danger, remove yourself from the situation before you try to analyze what has happened. Take a walk or time out in another room in order to get calmed down. Remember to let time pass and notice if you feel better just by letting some time pass.

3. Learn to observe yourself. Say to yourself, "I am reacting to an old feeling." Or say something to acknowledge what

is happening. "I am feeling angry as can be and I don't know why." Then ask yourself, "What in this situation might have caused me to overreact?" and "What is the original issue that is trying to be completed for me in this situation?" Your therapist can help you recreate the situation through role playing so you can access enough of the feelings and, yet, remain somewhat detached. Men should remember that anger often covers up sadness or fear, and women should remember that crying often covers up anger and fear. Look for the deepest feelings you can find.

4. Figure out what you need to do to take care of yourself in these situations. What do you want from your partner? How can you get your partner to cooperate with you to complete the process that you got stuck in long ago? Do you need to be held and comforted or do you need to check with your partner to see if his/her perception of what is happening fits with yours?

Tools for Support Groups

It is difficult to get clear of these patterns without support from friends. Having a network of friends who are willing to support your efforts to break free of the co-dependency trap is quite useful in completing this step in the recovery process. Friends frequently don't know what to do and feel left out if you are changing and not sharing your process with them. Some regular contact with friends can help you avoid slipping back into destructive patterns. If you don't have friends who will support your changes, you can use established support groups such as Co-Dependents Anonymous or Adult Children of Alcoholics.

Tools for Partnerships

Many times we literally hypnotize ourselves by the words we use to describe what we do. Our words can either trap us into co-dependent behavior or free us from it. The purpose of this partner exercise is to help each of you become more aware of those hypnotic word-blocks. "Have to" phrases tend to trap us and "choose to" phrases tend to free us.

- Each person individually should write a list of things that he or she feels he or she *has* to do to make the relationship work and, in turn, how he or she feels. Start each one with "I have to . . ." For example: "I have to do the laundry for the family and I feel burdened by this."

- Then sit facing each other, maintain eye contact and talk directly to each other. Take turns saying to each other the sentences you wrote on your list. Notice how you feel when you say each sentence. Partners need not make any response to comments but just accept what was said as true for that person.

- Now repeat the process, but this time change the beginning of the sentence to "I choose to . . ." Again pay attention to how you feel when you say each sentence and see if your feelings change as a result. Discuss the results with your partner. Ask yourself, "Am I allowing myself to be trapped by my own words?" Ask your partner, "Do I have to do this to please you or am I free to choose not to do this if I don't want to?" Also ask your partner, "Are you willing to choose and be responsible for your choices?"

- By changing your wording, you may also come up with alternative choices that you may not have thought of previously. The goal is to get to where you are consciously choosing your own life experiences rather than feeling controlled by your "have to" phrases.

The couple mentioned in the case example in the last chapter used this tool successfully to separate their lists and the control games that they had around their lists. Melvin went through his list of things that Dora had given him to do and decided which of those he felt he wanted to do and those he felt he had to do to please Dora. They renegotiated the ones that she wanted him to do but he didn't. They agreed to pay someone to do the chores that neither of them wanted to do. This was an option that neither had thought of before. Also, they agreed that in the future, Melvin would make his own lists of things he was willing to do and then check the list with Dora for input. This reduced considerably the control games between them.

Case Example

Jane was a bright, attractive single woman who met Jack and fell in love with him. They started living together and were planning marriage when Jane came to see me (Barry).

She explained that she loved Jack very much but she was disturbed about his drinking. She said that she grew up in an alcoholic home with an alcoholic father and didn't know whether she was just overreacting or whether there was a pattern emerging here. She also explained that she had been in several destructive relationships previous to this one where she discovered alcoholic behavior in the men she chose. So she was afraid to trust her own judgment.

After asking her some questions to find out more about Jack, I found out that he was resistant to therapy and anything that involved self-analysis or self-awareness. Jane really wanted a man who was willing to work with her to heal her own wounds and build a deeper, intimate relationship. She wanted to know whether or not she had picked the wrong person for that kind of relationship.

I suggested that she ask him to come to therapy with her for one session to help her determine what to do about the relationship. I said that this would be a way of determining how serious he was about that kind of relationship. She agreed and said she would let me know what happened.

The next day I received a call from Jane, who was in tears. She said she had asked Jack to come with her to therapy and he got so angry with her that he packed his things and moved out of their apartment, telling her he never wanted to see her again. She was shocked. As we talked, she calmed down and began to see how lucky she was that she hadn't gone ahead and married this man. She thanked me for helping her get clear on what she wanted and helping her find out Jack's level of commitment to the kind of relationship she wanted. I had one other session with Jane to help her see the early warning signals of co-dependency and alcoholism. She was still very gullible and knew that she had been attracting alcoholic and co-dependent men partly because she hadn't worked out her unfinished business with her father. She is now working on completing that unfinished business through a support group and by working on herself. At some point I expect she will return to therapy to work more on this process.

When you are not aware of how your co-dependent patterns relate to unfinished business from your past, it is very likely that you will subconsciously draw people into your life to help you complete these patterns. Obviously, in the case example above, when Jane met this man she had no idea how similar to her father he was. It was only when they had gotten close enough and were planning a more permanent relationship that she became aware of the similarity of patterns. Fortunately for her, she consulted with someone who could help her test out her fears. Many people don't become conscious of these patterns until they have been married for many years. Then it often takes them a long time to break free of the patterns or the relationship, if their partner is not willing to work on breaking the patterns.

CHAPTER TEN

I Have Met the Enemy and It Is I

Chapter Seven discussed the way that you had to develop a "false self" in order to please your parents and to support the denial that went on both in yourself and in your family. In developing this false self, you learned through interactions with your parents and other adults that certain parts of you were unacceptable to them, so you over-developed other parts of yourself that were acceptable to them. Joni is an example of a child who had to do this.

As a little girl, Joni liked being outside with the boys in the neighborhood, swinging on the ropes and racing on bicycles. These were behaviors of which her father and mother disapproved. Each time they found Joni outside behaving like a tomboy, they called her back inside to play quiet games with her sisters and to watch TV. Her father and mother made it clear to her that girls did not behave that way and what they wanted from her was quiet, passive behavior. Eventually she learned to repress this more outgoing, adventurous part of herself and adapted her behavior so that they would love her and approve of her. She became a nice, quiet girl.

As she grew older, she found herself irritated by some of the girls in her class who talked tough, entered competitive sports and acted adventuresome. Occasionally one of these girls would pick on her or ridicule her for her quietness, making her life miserable. She often felt helpless and defenseless in responding to their harassment. Joni was unaware of how much she envied these girls and their adventurous ways, seeing them more as strange and foreign.

The Enemy: Part of Myself

In understanding the dynamics of the situation just described, it is important to realize that you are made up of many different parts:

- the part that loves
- the part that hates
- the part that obeys
- the part that rebels
- the part that is happy
- the part that is sad
- the part that likes to control
- the part that likes to be controlled
- the part that is deceptive
- the part that is truthful
- the part that is feminine
- the part that is masculine
- the part that is an adult
- the part that is a child.

Each of these parts may have somewhat different desires, dreams, fears and ideas. These parts often behave like an internal family, competing against each other as they attempt to be recognized and get their needs met. For instance, your adult part may recognize that you need to get up and go to work in order to pay your bills, while your child part may want to stay home and ride your bike over to the park for a picnic. This sort of confict between parts is one we are usually aware of and can deal with effectively.

A more difficult situation occurs when you have a part of you that you don't like or that you think others might find unacceptable, such as the part of you that needs to receive love and affection. As a result of childhood experiences where you didn't get these needs met, you probably learned not to let people see this part of you. You may have stopped asking for and receiving affection. This part eventually became "split off" from your awareness.

Once a part has been split off, a strange thing begins to happen. People who have active parts similar to the ones you have split off will seem to come to trouble you in your life, as they did Joni. Whatever traits you refuse to recognize in yourself, you will begin to see in other people. If you have split off the part of you that needs to receive love and affection, you may find yourself surrounded by people who want love and affection from you. Or if you deny that you like being in charge and managing things, you may find a lot of people trying to manage and control you. "What you resist in yourself, persists."

The more completely a part is split off from your awareness, the more forcefully that part will come to meet you. When you meet this distant part of you in the form of another person, you may experience him or her as "the enemy." The enemy may appear in your life as a dominating boss, a shiftless employee, a distant wife or a rebellious child. You may find yourself embroiled in some persistent conflict with an enemy— perhaps a dominating boss, for example—and decide to switch jobs. Your new boss is easy to get along with but a co-worker whose desk is near yours turns out to be dominating. This phenomenon is called "projection."

Projection

Projection occurs when you see split-off parts of yourself in other people and don't recognize them in yourself. When you are projecting, you may have trouble distinguishing between your internal world and the external world.

Roger's difficulties around an impending separation and divorce are a good example of this phenomenon. He had been responding with calmness and grace to his wife's decision to leave him. Within one week, however, a series of catastrophes came one after another. It was not until a cat fell through the sunroof of his car and urinated on the back seat that he began to see the relationship between the *cat*astrophes of his external world and the *cat*astrophes of his internal world. He was able to see that the world was "pissing" on him and that he indeed was "pissed" that his wife was leaving him. He decided to deal with his anger toward her immediately.

Projection is complicated by the fusion of co-dependency and the inability to feel and act separate from other people. By seeing in others the very qualities that you refuse to acknowledge in yourself, you can avoid taking responsibility for your own feelings and for taking charge of your life.

Another important characteristic of split-off parts is that the more they are ignored or denied, the more strength they gain. They build energy until they reach a critical point. Then one of two things usually will happen.

1. You may act out the part unexpectedly. For example, if your anger is split off, you may erupt in a fit of anger. It "happens to you" without you having much awareness.

2. Someone may act out the part for you.

Split-off parts are always outside your awareness. If, for instance, you repress your anger and always try to be soothing or agreeable, you will experience yourself as a pleasant person. The people you interact with, however, may experience your anger in subtle ways. They may notice your tight jaw, frowning brows, pointed remarks, tense body posture or sharp tone of voice.

Men and women project their unclaimable parts on each other in relationships in a somewhat predictable pattern. We socialize men to develop their masculine parts and ignore their feminine parts, while the opposite is true for women who are taught to be feminine and not develop their masculine side. It is important to remember that both positive and negative parts can be projected. (It may be just as difficult to "own" your angelic parts as it is to own the more devilish ones.) In male/female relationships, there is a progression of projection of stereotyped parts that begins around puberty with the first attraction to the opposite sex and moves through a series of stages. Each stage involves a deeper level of distorted, stereo-typical projection and is more psychologically complex. The progression usually peaks by mid-life when people often be-come aware of their deepest projections. The progression for men and women generally follows this sequence:

Projected Feminine (Men)	*Projected Masculine (Women)*
The Shallow Woman	The Jock
Nurturing Woman	Big Daddy
The Madonna	Father God
The Goddess	The Hero
The Martyr	The Warrior
The Witch	The Warlock
The Wise Woman	The Sage

By mid-life, if there has been sufficient internal work through relationships, therapy, support groups and individual inner work, an integrative place is reached. If integration occurs, you will be conscious of your projections and the projections of others.

At the integrative level of development, each person is able to use any level of projection with awareness as a means of healing old wounds. For example, if you need more nurturing, you can ask your partner to temporarily become your projection of the Nurturing Woman and give you what you need. Being able to do this is an important part of reclaiming the true self.

Once you understand how people mirror your projected parts, it becomes easier to take back your projections. You just need to observe the people and behaviors that upset you. The people you once thought of as "the enemy" will change into "a lost part of yourself." Once you can do this, you are ready to begin loving yourself more fully.

Intimacy Begins With Loving Yourself

It is very difficult for us to accept our negative feelings like jealousy, greed, impatience, fearfulness or anger. Families usually provide little experience and few tools for dealing with these emotions. It is important to recognize that these parts also are useful and at times even valuable. Emotions such as anger and jealousy are valuable in protecting yourself. Chronic victims, for example, have a great need to be angry at their persecutors or victimizers so that they can prevent being abused or invaded. These parts are also useful in providing others with feedback about their behavior. Everyone needs to know how their behavior affects others. If you repress parts of yourself that give people information and feelings about their behavior, you deny them the consequences of their actions. Without feedback from others, it is very difficult to change dysfunctional patterns. It is important, both for yourself and for others, to love, accept and use with discretion *all* of your parts. In seeking split-off parts, you may discover them hiding somewhere inside.

Jerri, the oldest of six children, came to therapy suffering depression. In reviewing her childhood, it became clear that she "grew up too fast" and was assigned the role of surrogate parent to her younger brothers and sisters. Jerri shared several recent dreams where she was trying to kill a little girl. In working on the dreams, she discovered her own split-off child who felt as though she were dying. Further exploration revealed that in her dreams, Jerri was really trying to kill off this part of

her. She began to nurture her inner child by rocking herse
by taking time to play and by consciously allowing this part
come out more.

Loving your projections is the first step toward loving yourself. Only then will you be able to love others and live richly
in relationships.

Forgiveness

In the process of reclaiming your lost parts, you may discover
feelings of anger, hatred or resentment, especially toward your
parents or toward yourself. Finding such feelings and expressing them is an important part of healing these wounds. You
have good reason to feel these feelings. Only after you have
learned what really happened to you as a child that caused the
loss of vital parts of your real self, and felt the feelings connected
to this great loss, can you move into forgiveness.

True forgiveness does not deny the truth of your feelings or
deflect them. It faces them head on. It is especially important
that any feelings of hatred toward your parents be acknowledged. This is the path to true forgiveness. When your hatred
and anger are expressed completely (not necessarily to those
involved), they can be transformed into feelings of sadness and
pain at having been treated so poorly. This leads to the real
healing: a genuine understanding of your parents and why they
treated you the way they did. Only then can you begin to feel
the empathy and sympathy needed for true forgiveness of
them. It enables you to see *them* as victims—as people who
were responsible but not guilty. They did the best they could.
They need healing as much as you do.

A last part of forgiveness is to forgive yourself. It is important
to do this so that you don't create an internalized, abusive,
parental part and continue to mistreat yourself. If you find that
you are more critical of yourself than others, then you have
probably adopted an angry, hurtful, internalized parent. Forgiveness literally means to give back—"for-give." It is necessary to give back the traits of your parents that you don't want,
but have taken on.

Integrating Internal Parts

After you have identified lost or split-off parts, learned to love them, and forgiven yourself and your parents, the next step is to bring the parts together in your everyday life. Integrating these parts into your life will be useful in several ways. First, you will no longer need to defend against these parts when you see them in others and no longer need to idealize others. Second, you can now use these parts in productive ways to love or protect yourself or to get your needs met. Third, since many of these lost parts are connected to feelings, they will help you become a rich, full, feeling human being with a whole range of human responses to life.

For instance, if your ability to feel tenderness and compassion returns to you, you will be able to express these deep emotions when you experience intimate contact with someone. You will be able to express joy when something wonderful happens, such as receiving a warm letter from an old friend. When your child uses the car without asking and gets in a fender-bender, you will be able to get angry appropriately. When your spouse flirts at a party, you can state clearly that you feel jealous. All feelings become valued and have appropriate places for expression.

Once all your parts can be fully present in your life, you can begin to live a life richer than you ever imagined. You will find that the tension that you used to help you repress certain parts is gone. You begin to feel more relaxed and contented, and you will have a lot more energy. When feelings are allowed to surface in the moment rather than being repressed, your energy won't get trapped in your body. Your life becomes an authentic expression of who you are.

TOOLS FOR RECLAIMING LOST PARTS

Tools for Working Alone

- Have "parts days." As you dress each day, choose clothes that reflect different parts of yourself. Select clothes that really help you see the differences between your parts. For example, when you will be outdoors hiking, wear your boots, Western style shirt and a bandana. On special occasions, wear dressy clothes with jewelry or tie, fragrances, leather pumps or business shoes. On casual weekends, wear an exercise suit and sport shoes. Take time to reflect each day as you dress to go out in different parts. Write in your journal about these differences.

- Work on self-forgiveness. Write statements of self-forgiveness about the things you've been berating or beating on yourself about (e.g., "I now forgive myself for believing that I was a bad person."). Use a response column on the right side of each forgiveness statement to record any resistant thoughts and feelings about forgiving yourself (e.g., "I have done some pretty awful things."). Write responses for those forgiveness statements that you can complete without resistance. Then go back and work with your resistances. It may take a period of time to get through this exercise without resistances, so be patient with yourself.

Tools for Therapy

- "Prosecute" your parents with the assistance of your therapist. You may want to do this with each parent separately because their perceived "crimes" are frequently different. Stage a courtroom scene, asking your therapist to play the judge. You act as the prosecutor. Read a previously compiled list of things that you believe both parents did that hurt you or caused lasting wounds. Allow yourself to fully feel your rage and anger at their treatment. If necessary, imagine their faces on a pillow or bean bag and then pound on it. Yell at them until you are able to purge these old negative feelings out of your body. Following the prosecution, you will need to "defend" your parents. Again, your therapist can play the role of judge while you become the defense. In this process, you will act as different witnesses, including:

- your parents at different stages of their childhood

- the parents of your parents

- other people who played a significant role in your parents' childhood

- your parents as adults trying to raise you.

This exercise provides information about how they grew up, the difficulties and woundings they experienced and how that affected your childhood. Once this is done, it is easier to forgive your parents and yourself.

Tools for Support Groups

• Have a "parts party." Review your internal parts, listing as many of them as possible. Identify them by name, such as "my sexual part", "my child part", "my wife part", etc. Then think of a famous person who portrays that part to the point of exaggeration. For example, if your girl child part is precocious, wise and outspoken, you might portray her as "Edith Ann," the famous Lily Tomlin character. Or if you have a "preachy" part, you could portray it as "Billy Graham." Go to your group with your list and ask group members to take parts that match with their personalities. Then ask the parts to interact as "characters." For instance, "Edith Ann" would talk to "Billy Graham," while other parts talk in pairs or groups. After five minutes, have the pairs or groups switch to talk with new parts. Do this for a half hour or longer so that you can see the different ways your parts relate. During this role playing, notice any conflicts or inabilities to communicate between some of the parts. You should observe this whole scenario from outside the group. The parts should not interact with you. You should sit quietly at the edge of the group making notes about what you are seeing and how you are feeling. Stop the action when it has gone on long enough.

The next step is to let each person describe their experience as that part. Notice any information they give that might be useful for your self-awareness.

The last step is to have your group create a circle. Then put yourself in the middle of it. Look at each part (person) directly and tell it why you need it and what positive things it does for you. Then tell the part that you love it and will use it wisely. Do this with each part until you are completed. This last step is *very* important as it allows you to take back each part and integrate it into your daily life. It also allows the player to release the part so that they don't leave carrying your part around inside them. Co-dependent people are good at doing that.

- Have "parts nights." As a group, brainstorm the parts of yourself you have the most trouble accepting. Then make a list of the parts most common to the group. Make a schedule of the parts that you'd like to explore and rank order them 1,2,3,4, etc. Use each part as a theme for a meeting. Arrive at your group with everyone dressed in masks, outfits or costumes that portray this part. Use the meeting time to learn more about this troublesome part. You can draw what this part represents to you. You can also interact with other parts "players" in a theme drama. Use each other to help exaggerate your individual experiences. Use the last one-third of the meeting to discuss and share your experiences of this part.

Tools for Partnerships

- Make a list of all the things you wish your opposite sex parent had said to you or done for you. These are the things that you are still waiting for someone of the opposite sex to do for you. Decide which of the things you can do for yourself, which you would like to ask for from your partner and which you are willing to ask others for. Then ask your partner if he or she would be willing to do these items at a specific time.

- Review the list of masculine/feminine projections in this chapter. Then make a list of things your partner says or does that remind you of any of these parts. Share your lists with each other, using them as a discussion tool.

Case Example

Amy arrived at our office bruised and with fresh stitches around her eyes. Her loose teeth were wired to hold them in place while they healed. Her body was somewhat slumped as she walked in hesitantly and sat down. She held her head down and twiddled her fingers nervously as she began to tell the story of her near encounter with death.

She had been riding her bicycle near her home one evening about dusk and had stopped for a traffic light. Suddenly she felt both herself and her bicycle being dragged forcefully off the street and into a nearby parking lot.

Her assailant began beating her unmercifully about the upper body, face and head. She began screaming wildly and continued to scream and resist until she realized how much stronger he was. The blows dazed her so that she could scream and resist less. She knew that he planned to kill her.

Suddenly, another man ran up and scared the assailant off.

She was overcome with both relief and grief. The rescuer called the police and an ambulance and she was taken to the hospital emergency room for treatment. With information from the rescuer, the assailant was eventually caught and sent to prison.

For Amy, however, this was not enough. Amy believed that the attack was an important message for her. She believed that she had somehow drawn this experience to herself and wanted to explore what she might have done to make it happen. She wanted to focus her therapy on the lesson behind this incident.

Over a period of weeks, she shared a lot about the recent years of her life, especially about her relationships. One significant part of her story involved the breakup with her boyfriend. She also revealed a history of co-dependent relationships in which she was the attached person. As we pieced together a history of family relationships, her patterns became more clear.

Amy's parents were both severely dysfunctional. Her father was alcoholic and her mother was a multiple sclerosis invalid. Her mother died when Amy was ten. Amy, who was always closer to her father, clung to him even more after her mother's death. Her father, incapacitated from grief, soon became severely alcoholic. When Amy was seventeen, he shot himself.

Amy soon married an older man and had two children. After eight years, she divorced him and married again. This marriage also failed, so she stayed single even though she had several live-in relationships.

Just prior to her attack, she had been in a valued relationship with Larry. As their relationship became closer, all of their old feelings and issues from their past relationships and childhoods started surfacing. Both got frightened at the closeness of the relationship and the old feelings, which contributed to the breakup of the relationship. Following the breakup, Larry immediately found a new girlfriend to live with him.

Amy was devastated. She drove by Larry's house incessantly, often sitting outside to watch him and his new girlfriend. On several occasions, she got so angry she broke windows by throwing rocks through them. She banged on their door, shouting profanities and insults and attacking them whenever possible. She experienced moments when she was totally consumed by rage and hatred. She eventually cooled down and tried to resume a life on her own. It was at this point in her life that she was attacked while riding her bike.

Amy was able to see the similarity between her attack on Larry and the attack on herself. It became obvious to her and to us that the part she had split off was full of anger, rage and hurt and was expressing itself as an attacker. She also discovered that the breakup with Larry replayed the abandonment patterns with her mother and father. She admitted that she had not been able to express her rage and anger when they died. She believed, however, that she had released a lot of old feelings in her rage at Larry.

She became aware now of how she had split off this part for so long that it finally exploded in what she thought was a justified attack on Larry. It was only after her assailant had beaten her half to death that she was forced to look at her own "attacker" part.

She was eventually able to vent more of her anger at her parents for abandoning her and then reclaim her attacker part. She learned to deal with her feelings of anger more immediately and not them build up until they explode.

Amy's experience is an excellent example of how you can use people around you to show you what parts you may have split off. It is important to see the people you are involved with in conflict as symbols of your own internal parts. Recognizing them as parts of yourself allows you to work on the conflict internally and then to claim your part of it. The ability to work internally will noticeably reduce the way that you experience external conflict and also defuse the intensity of conflict situations.

CHAPTER ELEVEN

Eliminating Self-Hate

THE ROOTS OF SELF-HATE

Self-hate has its roots in the dominator culture. The first and most important cause of self-hate is related to the lack of support for independent thought and action. The second root is related to the Parental Disapproval Syndrome, a mechanism used by parents and teachers in a dominator culture to punish children for behavior that they do not like. The dominator culture uses rejection and disapproval as methods to control unwanted behaviors. This leads to the development of a negative self-image, low self-esteem, critical self-talk and self-hate. As a result of this repressive system, you learn to become a judgmental person, disapproving of others and of yourself. You will likely develop the same biases, prejudices, beliefs and values as your parents. You may also internalize your parents' beliefs and attitudes and end up criticizing, humiliating and abusing yourself long after your parents or teachers have stopped. Your internal dialogue or self-talk may even repeat the same words, phrases and name-calling that they heaped on you.

Black and White Thinking

Chapter Five presented information on the fourth stage of the separation process: object constancy. Object constancy—the ability of the child to see her or his parent and herself or himself as good and bad when they are separated—comes when the child has had enough "good parent" experiences to carry him or her through a period of separation. Lack of strong object constancy keeps the separation process or psychological birth from happening. As a result, the child stays stuck in this "splitting" stage where she or he will split the world into all-good and all-bad people and events. There are few or no gray areas. The dominator culture supports this dysfunctional form of thinking by using a comparative frame of reference.

If the child has poor object constancy and the parent is unavailable for any reason, both the child and the parent are seen by the child as "bad." The inability of the child to be separate from the parent causes the child to lump together feelings about the parent and himself or herself. This "bad parent = bad child" pattern creates all-or-nothing, black or white thinking and behaviors. It also creates a pattern of "bad child" that leads to self-hatred. When you make a mistake or fail to do something perfectly, this thinking will trigger all your negative thoughts and self-hate. Because it is difficult to be perfect and meet everyone's expectations, most of life can be lived out of "badness" and self-hate. Unless this is changed, it isn't possible to find self-love without becoming perfect. Since being perfect is next to impossible, people often cope in two ways. They may try to pretend they are perfect, or they have a need to be "right" about everything. The emphasis on winning and on "excellence," which very few people achieve in a dominator culture, serves to support failure and defeat as a way of life for most people.

Self-Love

Self-love begins when you are able to gain object constancy and see yourself as having both positive and negative parts that are all lovable. Self-love has been almost a taboo in our dominator culture, associated as it is with characteristics such as selfishness and masturbation.

Self-love, or self-nurturing, which is characteristic of partnership societies, is expressed in the daily relationship that you have with yourself. It is expressed in taking good care of your body through adequate exercise and plenty of rest, eating nourishing foods and using good grooming habits as well as wearing attractive clothing. Creating quiet time to meditate, pray and reflect supports loving your spiritual self. Going to therapy, finding community in support groups and spending quality time with your partner help you create harmonious social relationships.

Self-love, as it is expressed in your relationships with others, is evidenced by your ability to set appropriate boundaries. You can say *"no"* to abuse, to an invasion of your space, to being used, to drugs, to being controlled and manipulated, to guilt and to exposing yourself to negative people. "I'm worth it!" is an important attitude for self-love and may require that you be able to put your needs on an equal status with the needs of others. To begin loving yourself may require that you replace negative messages from your childhood so that you can create life situations where you experience acceptance and approval, high self-esteem, positive self-image and positive self-talk.

Self-Talk

Desire and fear are the two great motivators of the dominator culture. They can be used to propel or compel you to action. They are imbedded in advertising that is used to influence your thoughts, words and actions. You have been taught to think in words and phrases that you believe will affect your life either positively or negatively, depending on whether your dominant thoughts or self-talk are positive and based on desire or negative and based on fear. In either case, you may feel compelled to act in accordance with externalized standards, unable to really think for yourself.

Negative self-talk locks up your mental resources, your beliefs and your actions. Negative thoughts can form "brain chains" that run inside your mind like a continuous-loop cassette tape. They can have a devastating effect on your life by creating cycle after cycle of negative experiences. Positive self-talk, unless it is based solely on desire, releases your mental resources, beliefs and actions. It has a freeing, expanding effect on your life that helps create cycle after cycle of positive experiences.

The important thing about self-talk is that it fuels the performance cycle on which your actions are based. Self-talk creates beliefs. Beliefs create performance. Performance creates more self-talk.

In creating positive self-talk, it is very important to remember that you must move *toward* something. It must focus on the condition that you want to achieve rather than on what you want to move away from or what you fear or don't want. For instance, thinking to yourself, "I refuse to be co-dependent" is still focusing on the state of being co-dependent. Thinking, "I am interdependent" focuses on the concept of interdependency, your real goal.

Since the dominator culture accepts negative self-talk as its standard more than positive self-talk, it will take greater effort to get out of the negative self-talk habit. When someone offers you some of his or her negative thoughts, you may have to disagree with them mentally or internally and then create a positive self-talk statement to neutralize their negativity. For example, when your partner says, "This relationship is nothing but trouble," you can respond with, "Problems are an opportunity to get closer together." Positive self-talk supports positive self-esteem.

Self-Esteem

Self-esteem is the deep down, inside-the-skin feeling of your own self-worth. Positive self-esteem means accepting yourself, totally and unconditionally, fully realizing that you have strengths and weaknesses and positive as well as negative qualities. You are lovable without having to be perfect. To establish positive self-esteem, you need to concentrate on your positive attributes, your good qualities and your successes.

Self-esteem begins early in childhood. Because of the influences of the dominator society, it is estimated that between the ages of one and fifteen, children normally hear between 15,000 and 25,000 times, the words "no", "don't", "you can't", "better not" and "shouldn't." This kind of message from authority figures creates a base of negative self-talk that in turn creates limiting beliefs and limited performance. To neutralize this negative programming would require 15,000 to 25,000 "yeses", "you cans", "why nots" and "coulds." To create a base of positive self-talk requires another 15,000 to 25,000 positive messages!

The two most powerful tools for creating positive self-esteem are:

- asking for what you want and
- being willing to receive what you want.

If you have blocks in either area, you will have to work your way through them by giving yourself permission to have positive experiences.

Self-esteem affects the way that people interact in the world. According to Clemes and Bean (1981), people with high self-esteem:

- feel proud of their accomplishments
- act positively on their own behalf
- assume responsibility for doing their share
- tolerate frustration if things don't turn out as well as they would like

- approach new challenges with eagerness and enthusiasm
- feel able to influence their environment
- display a wide range of feelings.

People with low self-esteem:

- avoid difficult situations
- are easily led or deceived
- are defensive and easily frustrated
- don't know how they feel
- blame others for their own feelings.

Coopersmith (1967) found four components necessary for the development of positive self-esteem in children.

- *Acceptance of the child by adults, parents, teachers and other authority figures.* This helps reinforce bonding and create feelings of being valued.

- *Clearly defined and enforced limits.* These need to be as few as possible to help create a balance between experimentation and safety, exploration and invasion, and assertive and passive or aggressive behavior from the child.

- *Respect by adults for the child as a person.* It is important that the child's needs and wishes are taken seriously. This permits the child psychological space for growth and also for privacy and separateness.

- *Parents and other adults with high self-esteem as models.* Children need models to learn from. Also, adults with high self-esteem are better able to accept the child, to define and enforce limits and to respect the child as a person.

As an adult you may still need to work on these four things to maintain high self-esteem. You may still need acceptance, limits, respect and companions high in self-esteem. Self-esteem is also a developmental task, so you may need to find out where the self-esteem developmental task broke down and return to that point to repair it.

Affirmations

Affirmations are high-quality, positive statements that you make about yourself ("I am a lovable and capable person."). They can be written or spoken and should not contain any qualifiers such as "sometimes" or "under certain conditions," etc. They should also be stated in present time as if they have already happened ("I now weigh my ideal weight of 135 pounds.").

Affirmations are a special kind of self-talk that can be used to change the "tapes" that run inside your mind. When a situation occurs that has feelings, experiences or people that remind you of your unfinished business, you can get "rubberbanded" emotionally right back into the old stuff. The "old tapes" phenomenon helps this happen. For example, if a controlling older woman at work happens to criticize your work, you might flash back to a time from your childhood when your mother used the same tone of voice and facial expressions as she spoke to you. As a result, you may feel helpless to defend yourself and not know why.

Affirmations can be used to change any negative thought pattern. Once you have identified the negative thought pattern, you can convert it into something positive. Then you can "splice" this new "tape" into your internal tape player and replace the negative thought pattern with a positive pattern. With persistence, you can eventually edit out the negative messages and fill the tape with all positive affirmations.

Louise Hay (1984) uses affirmations, mirror work and support groups as primary tools for working with clients suffering from both cancer and AIDS. She has had remarkable results in healings with both patient groups. Many people go into re-mission after this kind of work. Her work also focuses on self-love, working with beliefs, and the relationship between self-love, beliefs and the incidence of illnesses.

TOOLS FOR LEARNING TO LOVE YOURSELF

Tools for Working Alone

• Take charge of improving your self-esteem. Find ways to im-prove your appearance, perhaps through exercise, diet, a change in hair style or new clothes.

• Listen to subliminal tapes that are designed to change your limiting beliefs about yourself and what you can achieve.

• Write personal affirmations using the following guides for writing and using them.

  – Be personal: say, "I"

  – Use the present tense: "I am"

  – State your change as a goal: "I am thin and healthy."

  – State your target clearly: "I am thin and healthy and I weigh 135 pounds and run two miles every other day."

  – Do your affirmations when you first rise each morning and just before going to sleep EVERY DAY!

  – Visualize the end result of your goal as having already happened when you say your affirmation.

  – Write your #1 affirmation on a notecard and carry it with you so that you can use it during free moments of your day.

Tools for Therapy

- Ask your therapist to do the first exercise in PARTNERSHIP TOOLS with you.

- Role play the process of changing negative self-talk statements into positive ones. Work with the negative comments about work, the weather or a person that you might find in more casual relationships.

- Discuss setting your own limits as a means of increasing self-esteem. Examine the issue of limits—how they were set and enforced in your childhood. Look for gaps or holes in completing that component of self-esteem. Create methods for completing the process.

Tools for Support Groups

- Group self-talk. If you have been together as a group long enough to know each other in more intimate ways, spend part of a meeting giving each other positive self-talk. Let one person be in the "love seat," while each person gives the recipient two or three minutes of supportive feedback. Allow time for the recipient to really take it all in.

- Find new options. Long histories of "brain chain" responses and negative self-talk can create the experience of limited options. Ask group members to volunteer information about situations where they have habitual responses and feel powerless to do anything else. As a group, brainstorm as many new options as possible for each member's situation.

Tools for Partnerships

- With your partner, create individual lists of things that you find are the most difficult to accept about yourself. Then write and share lists and discuss any feelings that come up. Then, one at a time, change the statements of difficulties into statements of acceptance ("I accept my growing baldness/wrinkles as a part of who I am."). Then read the statement of acceptance to your partner and have them affirm it: "I also accept your growing baldness/wrinkles as a part of who you are."

• Contract with each other to reflect instances when you hear your partner using negative self-talk and black and white words or statements. Listen for such words as "always" and "never" and statements that indicate "catastrophic thinking" ("Well, I guess it's all over. We may as well break up.").

• Discuss with your intimate partner sensitive self-love issues such as selfishness and masturbation. Explore your beliefs and feelings about separate interests, time alone and giving yourself sexual pleasure. These are areas where co-dependency often clings the strongest.

Case Example

Kate came to me (Janae) for therapy at a time when she found herself unable to make a decision about leaving her secretarial job. Her present job offered security, adequate pay, lots of stress and little opportunity for personal growth or advancement. A new job opportunity would pay about the same but offer less security. It would also be much less stressful and offer a lot of opportunity for personal growth and advancement.

Further exploration into Kate's background revealed a conflict between achievement and living a traditional feminine role. She had grown up in a rural area where most women lived very co-dependent lives. She'd had no feminine role models for becoming an achiever, even though her high school years had been full of accomplishments. Her strong drive for achievement seemed partly based on a deep need for parental approval and love. As the oldest child, she had experienced abandonment when the younger children had arrived. She had soon learned that achievements and counter-dependent behaviors won her some strokes and approval.

Kate's father and mother had given her two conflicting messages that seemed to be playing out in her job dilemma. The first message was, "Be an achiever and be independent if you want our love and approval." The second was, "Good women should take care of the people around them. They shouldn't be too smart or be selfish." Part of Kate felt that she should stay at the old job and take care of the dysfunctional people with whom she worked. She felt responsible for them and for her work duties. She was afraid to risk leaving her secure position and yet yearned for the possibilities of growth at the new position.

In therapy she discovered how she had put away vital parts of herself in order to gain love from her parents. She found it difficult to love herself and to believe in her own needs, dreams and ideas. This always created conflict with her other messages that she should serve others. As we worked on this dilemma together, I provided lots of mirroring and support for her achiever part, helping her to see that she could choose to do these things for herself as a form of self-love. I also shared my own story about having similar issues and how I had worked them through, to provide some role-modeling.

Kate worked diligently on herself to understand her family patterns and to express the feelings of anger and resentment at the double-bind or conflicting messages her parents had given to her. She did take the new job and within weeks was making leaps in self-esteem, as well as responding positively to the personal growth opportunities it offered.

Kate was also able to support her need for self-love and self-determination by reframing her history of frequent job changes from "lack of achievement" and "unstable" to "mastery at each job." She also saw herself on the path to involvement in global projects and was able to see each job as preparation for this global work. She returned to college and began to chart a much broader course for her life, continuing to create a feminine support system for herself and her new dreams.

CHAPTER TWELVE

Giving Up Power and Control Games

One predictable thing is that people who are co-dependent will try to control other people. The main ways they do that are by engaging in "one-up" or "one-down" power plays. They nag, scream, beg, bribe, protect, rescue, accuse, cry, run after, run away from, seek revenge, induce guilt, seduce, threaten, deliver ultimatums, pamper, whine, act hurt, lie, threaten suicide, lecture, insult, try to please, act helpless, hover over, complain, lock out, impress, condemn, bargain with, curse, threaten to kill, get drunk, wreck the car, throw things, break things, get sick, throw themselves on the floor, hide in a closet, talk about you behind your back, never admit they are wrong, leave, come back, leave again, drive recklessly, take drugs, overeat, work long hours, not get out of bed, tell people what to do, and what not to do, analyze, deny, project, rationalize, suppress, lock themselves in a room and anything else they can think of to *try to control the behavior of someone else*. The goal of all these behaviors is the same: to control another person.

Passivity: The Master Game of Co-dependency

Passive persons are masters at dominating and controlling the behavior of others from a "one-down" position. They know all the moves—the dominator culture has taught them well. Passivity is caused by the same thing that caused co-dependency: the failure to break the symbiosis or fusion with parents. Passive people behave the way they do because they never learned how to get what they want in direct, active ways. They use passivity to control others in order to maintain a co-dependent relationship. If we understand passivity and how it works, we can teach people to stop using passive behavior to try to get what they want. (Schiff 1975)

PASSIVE BEHAVIORS AND HOW TO CONFRONT THEM EFFECTIVELY

Behavior 1:

Do nothing. May say "I don't know" a lot when faced with a problem. May not answer questions. May engage in long silences before answering simple question.

Reasons for the Behavior:

They hope that you will do their thinking. They have learned that appearing weak and helpless got someone else to think for them.

How to Confront:

"I believe you have the information, so why don't you think about it and let me know what you want." "I expect you need to think." "If you need information that you don't have, you can ask for it." "Think about what you need from me (or others) and ask for it."

Behavior 2:

Overadaptation. Asking for over-detailed instruction. Compulsive attempts to please you.

Reasons for the Behavior:

People who use this approach are afraid to be wrong. As a result, they learned to do as they are told. They did not learn reasons for doing things and usually have faulty cause-effect thinking. They wish to give the responsibility for the problem to another person to solve so if the solution is wrong, they can't be blamed.

How to Confront:

"What are your reasons for doing that?" "People have reasons for doing what they do, and I expect you to think about what you want to do and why you want to do it." You need to make sure the person sets his or her own goals that take into account (1) what is appropriate for the situation, (2) his or her feelings and (3) other people's feelings.

Behavior 3:

Agitation. These are non-productive, repetitive behaviors (tapping a pencil, chewing on an eraser, pacing back and forth, talking incessantly without saying anything new).

Reasons for the Behavior:

Their behaviors are attempts to avoid solving a problem. They hope to wait out someone, anticipating that the other person will get uncomfortable enough to solve the problem.

How to Confront:

"Stop and think about what you want." "Instead of doing that, I want you to put energy into solving the problem."

Behavior 4:

Incapacitation or violence. These include temper tantrums, developing physical symptoms or fainting, having a seizure, etc. Or it could take the form of violence by kicking, hitting someone or breaking something.

Reasons for the Behavior:

This is a more desperate attempt to get someone else to take responsibility. Following the discharge of energy is a good time to help them to think and solve problems more effectively.

How to Confront:

Take whatever steps are necessary to restore order or control. The person is out of control and at that point taking control is a very direct and appropriate way to confront them. Following the blow-up: "It is not okay for you to solve problems that way." "Think about what you could have done differently to solve the problem." Immediately *after* a blow-up is the best time to get them to do some new thinking about the problem. Just before or during a blow-up, this response usually doesn't work.

How to Avoid Rescuing

One of the most important interpersonal communication challenges for co-dependent people is to recognize and avoid rescuing. Every situation in which one person needs help from another is potentially a situation in which one person can become a Rescuer and another person can become a Victim. This is how the dominator culture maintains "one-up—one-down" relationships. Rescuers maintain one-up power by doing something, without being asked, for another person that they were perfectly able to do for themselves. It carries implied messages such as "I can do it better than you" or "You can't do it for yourself." The Victim usually feels the subtle put-down and then may become a Persecutor and get angry at the Rescuer, enabling him or her to become a Victim as well ("I was only trying to help."). What helps keep this going is competition for the Victim role, which is the only way for many people to get needs met in a dominator culture.

The ways to avoid rescuing your partner are as follows:

- Don't help your partner without a verbal contract. ("What do you want from me?")
- Don't ever believe that a person is helpless (unless he or she is unconscious). ("I know you can solve that problem. Let's discuss it further.")

- Help people who are feeling helpless to find ways in which they can identify and apply the power they have. ("Think about some ways you could solve that and then talk to me.")

- Don't do more than 50% of the work on the problem or task; require that your partner do at least 50% of the work at all times. ("This is what I'm willing to do—What are you willing to do?")

- Don't do anything you don't really want to do. ("No, I'm not willing to do that.")

The Rescuer acts superior to the Victim. The role of the Victim is to be powerless and inferior in relation to the Rescuer. Behaving in either of these two roles inevitably leads to accumulated feelings of resentment that will eventually lead one into the Persecutor role. The intensity of the Persecutor role usually will be in direct proportion to the intensity of the Rescuer or Victim role you have played. The ways to avoid Persecuting your partner are as follows:

- Avoid behavior that unnecessarily places you in a one-up position. Avoid talking down to your partner or giving advice unless it is requested. Don't interrupt people. Maintain equality in all spheres except where you have more experience and expertise. Strive to reduce any inequality by sharing everything you know about the subject with your partner.

- If you feel angry at your partner, check to see if you have rescued them by having done more than 50% of the work. Also check to see if you did something you didn't want to do and didn't say anything about it for fear of hurting your partner's feelings. Examples of this are: listening to people when you are bored, continuing to do something when it feels unproductive, doing things you don't want to do either because you don't like the person, he/she bores you or you are tired. The responsibility is half yours. The more angry you are at your partner or the more angry he/she is at you, the more you are likely to have rescued or persecuted him or her. Remember, there is no such thing as a person playing a game with you unless you are being a full partner in it. If you get angry at your partner often (more than once a week), look to see what *your* part in the problem is and decide what to do about it.

- Don't allow feelings of resentment to accumulate in your partnership. Share held resentments as soon as possible and encourage your partner to give constructive feedback to you.

- Don't invite persecution or rescue from your partner. Some people, in order not to be one-up, come from one-down. This can be done by dressing sloppily, being sick a lot, not keeping agreements or by being passive.

- What keeps this game going is competition for the Victim role. Many people believe this is the only way they can get their needs met. To break this game, you will need to be willing to ask for what you want 100% of the time and to learn to negotiate the differences.

One-Up/One-Down Power Moves

The following list identifies some of the common power moves that co-dependent people make in an attempt to dominate or control the behavior of their partner.

- *Poor timing.* Pick a fight during a favorite TV show, or just as your partner is going to sleep or is leaving for work. The idea is to keep your partner off balance and limit his or her ability to respond.

- *Escalating.* During an argument, move from the topic and start questioning your partner's personality or make statements that distract your partner. Use phrases like "you always" or "you never."

- *Sand bagging.* Throw in as many problems as you can think of. Dig up old conflicts and show how they might be related.

- *Asking why.* "Why didn't you . . .?" or "Why were you so terribly late?" This puts the other person on the defensive immediately.

- *Blaming.* Blame it all on the other person. You are right, they are wrong and how come they won't admit it?

- *Pulling rank.* Rather than standing on the merits of your argument, remind your partner that you have more education, money or experience.

- *Labeling.* Label your partner's behavior as childish or neurotic or co-dependent. This is a common way to obscure the issues where you feel shaky.

- *Leaving.* This prevents any resolution of a problem. You can walk out of the room, leave the house, just refuse to talk or threaten to leave.

- *Avoiding responsibility.* Saying you don't remember or you must have been drunk or too sleepy can prevent resolution of a conflict.

- *Playing martyr.* By going into hopelessness, you can use one-down power to manipulate your partner. You could say, "Yes, you're always right; I am a hopeless case," or you can threaten to kill yourself if your partner doesn't shape up.

- *Using money.* This is a common way to control a spouse. The old favorite is: "When you make as much money as I do, then you can complain."

TOOLS FOR GIVING UP POWER AND CONTROL GAMES

Tools for Working Alone

There is a six-step assertiveness process (Bolton 1979) that is helpful in breaking power and control games. It works this way:

1. *Prepare yourself.* The first step in preparation of a clear, assertive message is to write it and review it. Make sure that

- it doesn't invade the space of the other person
- it is a persistent concern
- you have built a base of trust
- you can get your needs met by sharing this message.

Obtain an appointment to deliver the message and choose neutral ground, if possible. Timing is important, so avoid times when people are tired or rushed.

2. *Send your message.* Communicate your message directly, maintaining eye contact. Breathe fully, using a calm yet firm voice.

3. *Be silent.* Wait a while after communicating your message to allow the other person to think about the message and to speak what is on his/her mind.

4. *Active listening defensive responses.* If your partner starts to defend, you will need to shift gears and actively listen to the other person's defensive response. ("You are feeling wrongly accused of that" or "You seem hurt by what I said.")

5. *Recycle process.* You will need to restate your message, follow it with silence and listen again to any defensiveness until you get the feeling that your partner understands your message. It typically takes from three to ten repetitions to get to this point. Persist.

6. *Focus on the solution.* This is usually a negotiation process. You must ask the other person for what you need and then be willing to negotiate the conflict until both people are satisfied with the solution. When you have agreed, restate the agreement to make sure you both understand. Also arrange some way to check with each other to make sure the solution is working. This is important to assure that neither of you agrees to something you find won't work.

Tools for Therapy

Control and power games arise out of poor self-esteem and weak object constancy. Therapy can help you develop a program to improve your self-esteem. There are four main skill areas that determine your level of self-esteem. (Weinhold 1983) They are:

1. *Contact skills.* People with high self-esteem make effective contact with themselves and others.

2. *Acceptance Skills.* People with high self-esteem accept differences between themselves and others. They respect the right of others to be different, and they take seriously their own feelings and behaviors, even when they are different from others.

3. *Influence skills.* People with high self-esteem make things happen for themselves and others and effectively stop unwanted things from happening.

4. *Constancy Skills.* People with high self-esteem maintain a fairly constant positive self-image or good feeling about themselves even in the face of failure.

Complete the "Self-Esteem Questionnaire" at the end of this chapter to help you determine the areas with which you need help in therapy. A good therapist should be able to develop a plan to help you shore up any weak skill areas.

Tools for Support Groups

Support groups can provide you with an opportunity to rehearse a scene in which you have trouble maintaining your position or staying out of game behavior. One of the most difficult situations for a co-dependent is when they have to say "no." They often need the support of others in developing effective ways to say "no" when they need to. By role playing or rehearsing a situation where a resolute "no" is called for, you can strengthen your ability to stay out of co-dependency. Some effective ways to say "no" are as follows:

- *The reasonable "No."* When you say *no*, give a very clear and succinct reason for your response. In answer to a request to go out drinking with the boys, you might say, "No, thanks. I no longer go out drinking. I am serious about staying with my 12-step program."

- *Active listening, then "No."* First you respond to the request and then you say *no*. For example, if your partner wants to go to the movies and you want to watch TV, you might say, "You look like you were really counting on me going to the movies with you tonight. Is that correct?" Then follow it with, "I'm sorry, but I would like to watch my favorite TV show tonight. Would you be willing to go without me this time?"

- *The raincheck "No."* Here you can say *no* for now but request that you be asked again. Your partner asks you to cook dinner tonight and you have plans to go to a meeting. You can say, "I have plans tonight but I would be willing to cook tomorrow night. Is that acceptable?"

- *Broken record.* This is useful in cases where people refuse to take *no* for an answer. In these cases, you may need to develop a one-sentence refusal statement and repeat it over and over like a broken record, no matter what the other person says. ("I don't have any money to loan you.") It is good to develop your statement ahead of time and rehearse it if possible so that you can continue to hold your ground while you repeat your message.

Tools for Partnerships

- Game-breaking responses can make it easier for partners to get out of power and control games. Such responses make it hard for the other person to continue the game. Two very effective game-breakers are: "Thank you, I wasn't aware of that" and "Thank you, I am aware of that."

- It is also important that partners set ground rules for handling conflict. The following are five conditions that are necessary for the establishment and maintenance of a cooperative relationship (Steiner 1974):

  1. *No scarcity.* There has to be a belief that both people can get what they want if they cooperate with each other.

  2. *Equal rights.* Both parties have to agree that they each have equal rights to getting their needs and wants satisfied and share equal responsibility for creating a cooperative relationship.

  3. *No power plays.* Both parties must agree to enter into problem-solving and not use a power play or game to get what they want.

  4. *No secrets.* Both parties have to agree to be honest with each other and not keep secrets.

  5. *No rescues.* Both parties have to agree not to do things for each other without asking. Both agree to ask for what they want and to negotiate differences.

Case Example

A conflict that Dora and Melvin brought to couples therapy provides a good example of how to stop power and control games. They were at an impasse on a conflict around Melvin's driving habits. Dora was critical of his driving habits, claiming that she was afraid to ride with him anymore. The more Dora criticized, the more Melvin resisted and denied her accusation. Finally he said that he would not drive anymore. He insisted that Dora had to drive from now on. She had agreed reluctantly and wanted to find a better solution. Melvin agreed to discuss it only in therapy. Specifically, Dora accused Melvin of drifting out of his driving lane and not looking properly when he wanted to change lanes. She claimed that they nearly had two accidents recently because of his inattentive driving habits.

By helping Dora rephrase her message and by reflecting Melvin's feelings, we were able to get them to a place where they could explore possible solutions. We also found that Melvin frequently needed Dora's help when he wanted to change lanes in heavy traffic because of a blind spot in their car. However, he did not ask her for help because she frequently was knitting or reading while they drove. He tried to do it himself and did admit that it was difficult for him to see around the blind spot. He agreed to ask her to help him when they got in traffic, and she said she would be delighted to help if she were asked.

One additional problem remained and that was Melvin's tendency to drift out of his lane. He admitted that sometimes he did let his mind drift off of his driving and that the car might drift over if he wasn't paying close attention. He said that happened occasionally on the open highway. Dora said that when the car started to drift she got scared and often would yell at Melvin to bring him back. He objected to her yelling at him to get his attention. It made him feel bad and often led to a fight between them. What we found was that Dora and her family had been involved in a bad automobile accident when she was a child and that had traumatized her. No one was killed, but she and several other family members were injured. She said she still has fear of that happening again. Melvin, on the other hand, never was in an accident and tended to react to Dora's fear as if she were telling him he didn't know how to drive. Dora's comments reminded him of his critical mother.

We looked for a better way for Dora to make contact with him, should he want her assistance in driving. What Melvin thought would work would be for Dora to reach over and touch him on the arm when she started to get scared and say, "Melvin, I am getting scared. Would you focus more attention on your driving?" He was delighted with the solution.

Dora and Melvin developed a cooperative rather than a competitive way to handle driving and recognized that this way of cooperating could actually bring them closer together while they were driving. Melvin said, "I may even enjoy driving again," as he smiled at Dora. As they drove away from the session, we noticed that Melvin was again at the wheel.

Because people aren't taught effective, healthy ways to get their needs and wants met, they rely on less effective, dysfunctional ways to get them met. All of these less effective and dysfunctional ways involve the use of power plays, control and manipulation and take their toll on relationships. These games can produce lots of conflict in relationships and cause people to feel stuck. Terminal stuckness in a relationship occurs when you believe that you have to wait for someone else to change in order to feel better. This description is characteristic of what happens in many co-dependent relationships.

AWARENESS ACTIVITY

The "Self-Esteem Questionnaire" that follows may help you locate the specific areas where your self-esteem may be weak. Fill it out, score it and then see if you can develop a plan for improving yourself in one or more areas.

SELF-ESTEEM QUESTIONNAIRE
(WEINHOLD 1983)

Rate each of the items below from 1 to 4, depending on how consistently you are able to perform each behavior.

> 1 = I am hardly able to do this.
> 2 = I am sometimes able to do this, but I still strongly need to increase my capacity here.
> 3 = I can do this fairly often, but feel I could improve in this area.
> 4 = I can do this often and in a manner with which I am satisfied.

Area A: Contact Skills
____ 1. I am able to ask for help or can ask someone for something I need, without feeling inadequate or guilty.

_____ 2. When I'm with another person, I feel fully there. My thoughts don't drift away to other things.

_____ 3. When I talk to others, my words and voice match how I feel.

_____ 4. I take an active part in groups and enjoy being involved.

_____ 5. When I like someone, I can show them directly how I feel.

_____ 6. I can be aware of how my body feels, what parts are tense, when I need rest, etc., and seriously try to follow what my body tells me it needs.

_____ CONTACT SUB-SCORE

Area B: Acceptance Skills

_____ 1. I can express my ideas without waiting to hear what other people think.

_____ 2. I can go with my feelings and let myself experience them as an important part of me without getting stuck with or hanging onto any particular feelings.

_____ 3. I take time to show my own taste and interests in such things as how I decorate my office, how I dress and how I express myself. The expressions of myself in these areas are more important than what others will think of me.

_____ 4. There are times I choose to be alone, to withdraw from others and be by myself—resting, loafing or doing something I enjoy. At these times I do not feel I have to be productive.

_____ 5. I take time to do imaginative and creative projects.

_____ 6. I can share my point of view even when others differ with me.

_____ ACCEPTANCE SUB-SCORE

Area C: Influence Skills

_____ 1. I can handle a great deal of pressure without stomach upset, headaches, etc.

_____ 2. I am able to set firm and clear limits for myself and others without trying to make either myself or the other person guilty.

_____ 3. I can express my feelings appropriately without feeling I'm losing control.

_____ 4. I seek responsibility and enjoy being in charge of projects and activities.

_____ 5. I can make decisions without excessive delay or stress.

____ 6. I can take risks in new situations and find them challenging and exciting.

____ INFLUENCE SUB-SCORE

Area D: Constancy Skills
____ 1. I feel okay even when others disapprove of what I do.
____ 2. I can admit my mistakes.
____ 3. I can listen to positive and negative feedback from others without feeling embarrassed.
____ 4. I can tell the truth about my perceptions even when others might not agree with me.
____ 5. I feel okay about myself even when things I plan don't work out for me.
____ 6. I can turn disappointments into new challenges.

____ CONSTANCY SUB-SCORE

____ TOTAL SCORE

Scoring: Add the numbers for each answer. Use the following chart to interpret your scores.

24-48 low self-esteem in most areas of your life
49-72 low self-esteem in a few areas of your life
73-96 high self-esteem in most areas of your life

CHAPTER THIRTEEN

Learning to Ask for What You Want

Most co-dependents have poor communication skills. Along with "don't think or feel" messages in childhood came "don't ask for what you want" messages. As a result, co-dependents have to carefully choose words that help them manipulate and control, please people, cover up and remain passive in order to get what they want. Co-dependent communication is full of repressed thoughts, ulterior motives, repressed feelings, low self-esteem and shame. Co-dependents learn to act happy when they're not. They justify, rationalize, compensate and deceive. They may also badger, threaten or be unassertive. Often, the message is, "If you really loved me you would figure out what I need and give it to me. If I have to ask, then I can't trust whether what you give me comes from love or is just another way of manipulating me."

Co-dependents are indirect, not able to say what they mean or mean what they say. They hope that someone will read their mind, and they work hard at reading the minds of others. All of this, of course, supports the Victim role on the Drama Triangle, as well as the one-up/one-down power plays.

Underlying this passivity is the infantile dream that mother or some other nurturing figure will just *know* what the co-dependent's needs are. They can go through their whole life using this indirect way of communicating and, as a result, never get their real needs met.

To make the shift from indirectness to directness in your communication, you may need to replace some of your negative self-talk with positive self-talk that will support you in asking for what you want. Some key positive concepts include:

- It is important to ask for what you want.
- Who you are is okay.
- Your feelings and thoughts are okay.
- It is acceptable to talk about yourself and your problems.
- Your opinions count.
- Sometimes you need to say no.
- Telling the truth sets you free.

Once you create beliefs that support these concepts, asking for what you want becomes much easier.

ASSERTION SKILLS

Experts estimate that less than 5% of the population can communicate assertively. (Satir 1972:78-79) Though this is presently shifting, approximately 95% of the population is not getting its needs met and little of importance transpires in the day-to-day communication of the dominator culture.

Assertiveness is the ground between submissiveness and aggressiveness. It allows you to communicate in ways that enable you to maintain your self-respect, pursue your goals, satisfy your needs and defend your rights and personal space, without dominating or manipulating others. The assertive person stands up for his or her own rights and expresses personal needs, values, concerns and ideas in direct or appropriate ways.

Knowing What You Want

Wants differ from needs. Needs are the physical and psychological conditions necessary for safety and survival, while wants are things or conditions that you desire but can live without. If you confuse needs and wants, you can confuse issues of safety and survival with issues of comfort. You can also have trouble establishing priorities when you have choices to make.

Messages to "not think" and "not feel" also prevent co-dependents from reflecting on their inner experience. This literally trains them out of knowing what they want and makes learning to be assertive more difficult. You may need to do a lot of journaling to help you discover the differences between needs and wants and to learn what your needs really are. Co-dependents are used to adapting to the needs and wants of others and ignoring their own, so you will want to monitor yourself for adaptive behavior.

Confrontation

Confronting or asserting firmly may be necessary to protect yourself, to get your needs met or to point out discrepancies in what people say or do. Confronting usually is used in sensitive areas and between people who have a contract for doing that, or in threatening situations when there is invasion. Confrontation quickly engages the confrontor and confrontee in interaction, so a good rule to follow is that you "Only confront people you want to get closer to or people who are invading your space without permission."

Asking For What You Want:
A Nine-Step Process

HOW TO ASK FOR WHAT YOU WANT

1. Describe objectively the problem or behavior. ("When you get angry and yell and scream . . .")

2. Share your feelings about the problem or behavior. ("I feel scared like I did when I was little and Dad yelled at me.")

3. Describe the effects or results of the problem or issue on you and/or your relationship. ("I want to run away from you and hide.")

4. Pause for a moment to listen to the other person's feedback or perceptions about the conflict. Do not allow yourself to get bogged down at this step in defending, blaming or escalating. Stop only long enough to listen to short feedback.

5. State clearly what it is you want from the other person. ("What I want from you is for you to express your anger in words like, 'I am angry.' ")

6. Ask the person clearly, "Would you be willing . . . ?" ("Would you be willing to say that you are angry without yelling and screaming at me?")

7. Negotiate if there are differences between what you want and what the other person is willing to give or do. ("I need to let off steam when I feel angry. I would like to be able to raise my voice.") and ("I can handle your raising your voice if it doesn't turn into yelling and screaming and if you don't direct it at me.")

8. If you are unable to negotiate the differences, agree to disagree. ("I see that we just don't agree on this issue and I accept our disagreement. Will you also agree to disagree?")

9. If the differences are unresolvable and the relationship ends, mark it with some ceremony of completion. Write a letter stating your perception of your unresolvable differ-

ences without blame, seeing yourself and the other person as okay. You may choose to either mail it or perhaps burn it.

The above guide will help you learn to ask for what you want. The first three steps, which involve thinking, feeling and reflecting, are not enough. If you stop here, you will not get your needs met. It is likely that you will just sound like a complainer. Steps four through seven involve doing. They require that you state clearly what you want and then ask for it. They also encourage negotiation to settle differences. Step eight offers you a way of resolving a conflict with someone who refuses to work on the conflict. There are instances when the "agreement to disagree" leaves you feeling incomplete, so step seven allows you to complete your part of the conflict and move on with your life.

When Conflict Results

If you have been a passive or adaptive person and you begin asking more clearly for what you want, you may find yourself in conflict more often. Conflict is often associated with fighting, compromising, losing, rejection and humiliation—all negative concepts. It is considered the opposite of the romantic love that is full of idyllic days and nights, unmarred by bickering or unpleasantness. As a result, most people avoid conflict and try to create the romantic dream that Hollywood portrays in movies.

Conflict is not inherently bad. In fact, it can be a constructive force and bring positive elements into a relationship if you have skills at working through conflicts. Taking a positive attitude toward conflict is helpful because it is unavoidable unless the partners have exactly the same needs, wants and dreams. How you handle conflict is more important than the context of the conflict. There are three main ways to deal with conflict: defend, deflect or discover.

Defending is used to protect yourself from harm or threats of harm. When defending, it is important that you are careful to meet the attack with an amount of force exactly equal to the force of the attack. This will neutralize the attack. If you respond with just a little more energy, you will cause the other person to escalate the conflict and prolong it. If you meet the attack with just a little less energy, you may encourage additional attack and set yourself up to get victimized. Either of these last responses can elicit or create one-up and one-down power plays.

Deflecting a conflict may also be necessary in some cases. If you are being attacked by someone coming at you with the force of a freight train, you need to jump off the track. If your partner in a conflict flips into a rage state or a moment of temporary insanity, the best response is to leave until they have cooled down. Deflecting is also useful in responding to people who have a pattern of hooking you into conflict and then refusing to work it through with you.

Discovery creates an opportunity to learn more about your partner. It can be a time to explore parts or aspects of them that have been unknown to you. Discovery is also an opportunity to learn about yourself. Sharing with your partner and taking in feedback from him or her may reveal parts or aspects of yourself that previously have been projected or are outside your awareness. This kind of mutual "uncloaking" is very common when couples decide to discover. In discovery you can stop blaming and assume responsibility for your behavior. It becomes safe to be open and vulnerable, to risk feeling and expressing your old pain and wounds. When the defensive walls come down and conflict becomes a cooperative matter, real intimacy can begin.

Conflict As Intimacy

If conflict is really an opportunity for intimacy, then perhaps a new definition of intimacy is needed. Intimacy is usually associated with romance and pleasantness. Conflict can also be quite intimate. In the midst of conflict, people are usually expressing their feelings, so these moments feel more *real* even though they also may be unpleasant. Conflict also can knock down defenses so that hidden parts of people get exposed. With these parts often come old feelings and old wounds wanting to be healed. When you reach this point in partnership, another kind of intimacy is possible. Being present to hold and support your partner in such a vulnerable moment creates a sacred space between you. Intimacy becomes a broad concept that includes those typical romantic experiences as well as experiences of anger, sadness, grief and discomfort. If you can expand your view of intimacy to include all the experiences of your relationship, you will find yourself able to feel close, even when you are in conflict.

Most people fear conflict because it causes feelings of separation. As you are able to complete your psychological birth and work through the resolution of oneness and separateness issues, you will find conflict less frightening. You will also find that reframing intimacy into this larger perspective becomes easier.

TOOLS FOR LEARNING TO ASK FOR WHAT YOU WANT

Tools for Working Alone

- Write in your journal about your needs and wants. Make one list of things you *need*. List them in the order of their importance. Decide how you will meet these needs. List the things that you *want* in the order of their importance. Decide what you are willing to do in order to fulfill these wants.

Tools for Therapy

- Contract with your therapist to work on assertiveness. Decide what issues around assertiveness you want to work on (passivity, phrasing requests, learning to say "no"). Decide who are the most difficult people to confront in your life. Describe them to your therapist and ask him or her to role play them while you practice your confrontation skills. Ask your therapist for feedback about your effectiveness and for suggestions on improving your skills. List your most common conflicts in relationship. With your therapist, review them to identify patterns and look for their sources. Develop effective ways to resolve them.

Tools for Support Groups

- Discuss the kinds of conflicts that you all had growing up in each of your families and list them by category (child-rearing, money, work, addictions, etc.). Then pick one to reenact together. Ask one member to be the objective observer or facilitator to monitor the reenactment. Have the observer stop the action every five minutes to check how people are feeling and to suggest new responses to old patterns.

- Contract as a group for people to ask for what they want. Watch group interactions for rescues, manipulation, victim responses, complaining and making assumptions without checking them out. When you hear someone complaining, ask them directly, "What is it you want?" This stops people from using complaining as a way to manipulate.

Tools for Partnerships

Discuss with your partner how you each go about resolving conflicts. Include such things as:

- ways that you defend (blame, denial)
- ways that you attempt to change others or control them (anger, threats, withdraw love, criticism, nagging, sarcasm)
- ways that you become indifferent (work, TV, reading, sports, hobbies, meditation)
- resisting and then rebelling after your partner makes the decision.

Evaluate together a recent conflict with each other. Ask your-selves these questions:

- What did I want from the conflict?

- What did I get from it?

- Did I ask clearly for what I wanted?

- Was I able to ask for what I wanted in such a way that my partner was delighted to give it to me?

- Were we able to negotiate our differences?

- Were we able to fight clearly?

- Did either of us hurt the other?

- Did I learn something new about my partner or about myself in the conflict?

- Did I reveal something new about myself to my partner?

- What would I do differently?

- Did we end up feeling closer at the conclusion?

Case Example

Raymond is a classic example of a man who cannot ask for what he wants. Growing up in a reserved family, he had no models for learning this skill. He coped with this inability by marrying Mary Ann, who was well-trained in "mind reading" and taking care of the wants and needs of others. She trained their three daughters with regard to his food preferences, his daily habits and how to anticipate his physical needs. Both his wife and daughters became adept at observing his non-verbal signals. They would refill his water glass or pass him food before his glass or plate was empty.

Raymond also could get his emotional needs met without asking for what he wanted. When his wife or a daughter failed to take care of some physical need sufficiently, he would ex-plode in anger. Intimidated by his anger, they would repent and pledge to do better. Then they could all hug him and feel close.

This is a life pattern that Raymond is unwilling to change. As a result of his addictions to food, work and power, he has had to maintain superficial relationships with everyone. His inability to express his needs, his addictions and his lack of self-esteem are evidenced by his poor physical health and growing state of obesity.

Not everyone is willing to work through their addictive patterns. Sometimes the pain of recovery and the effort required to learn more effective ways of living and relating seem too much to cope with.

CHAPTER FOURTEEN

Learning to Feel Again

Co-dependency is a feeling disorder. Co-dependent people are out of touch with their true feelings. The only feelings they allow themselves to express are what are sometimes called "racket" feelings. These are feelings of anger or sadness that have been justified in the mind of the co-dependent as being caused by the actions of someone else: "She made me so angry" or "He made me cry." Because co-dependents have a need to discharge pent-up emotions, they have to manipulate or blame someone in order to get their feelings out. These racket feelings are also used to cover up deeper and more genuine feelings.

WHAT ARE FEELINGS?

By growing up in a culture that still is largely oriented to a dominator model, we know very little about feelings. We have over-emphasized our rational thinking functions and have virtually ignored the feeling function. Most Americans don't even know what their basic feelings are for. Carl Jung said, "The feeling function is the reason of the heart which the reason of the mind does not quite understand." (von Franz and Hillman 1979)

There are five basic feelings, each with many variations that are based on intensity. The basic feelings are as follows.

BASIC FEELINGS AND DEFINITIONS

Feeling	Definition
1. Anger	A natural response to not getting your wants/needs met. You may not give yourself permission to express anger and feel scared to express it.
2. Fear	Your natural response to perceived physical or emotional danger. You may not have permission to think and feel at the same time. You may use fear to cover anger.
3. Sadness	Your natural response to the loss of a person, thing or relationship (real or fantasy). It is an important part of "giving up" something you are attached to. There may also be some anger connected with the loss.
4. Excitement	Your natural anticipation of something good happening. Fear and excitement are closely related. Some children don't have permission to show excitement.
5. Happiness or Joy	Your natural satisfaction at getting what you want or need, or for doing something effectively. Some people don't know it's acceptable to be effective and be happy.

Some people use other words as feelings, and these often become ways to avoid the basic feelings or to justify behavior. Words like "frustrated", "guilty", "hurt", "annoyed" or "irritated" are usually covering anger. Words like "confused", "nervous", "uneasy" or "tense" cover fear. Sadness is often expressed as "lonely", "bored", "empty" or "low." Some words represent a combination of feelings. "Depressed", "unhappy" or "upset" can be a combination of anger, fear and/or sadness. Suffering is usually anger and fear operating in a person who doesn't have permission to express these emotions. It is important to correctly identify your own basic feelings and learn to make use of them in your decision making.

Feelings are natural, normal responses to your experiences. They can help you form your values and make decisions. You learned very early in life to begin to distort your feelings. Elizabeth Kübler-Ross expressed it this way: "We all start out perfect. You begin to see that people become twisted when their natural emotions are suppressed." (Zaleski 1984:41) Alice Miller (1983) writes that we stay stuck in infancy and co-dependency because:

- We had our feelings hurt as a small child, without anyone ever noticing our hurt feelings.

- Then we were told not to be angry at being hurt.

- Then we were forced to show gratitude toward those who hurt us because they had good intentions (they didn't mean to hurt us).

- Then we were told to forget everything that happened.

- Finally, we were shown how to get rid of our stored-up anger by being violent and abusive toward others who were smaller or weaker than us, or we were told to direct that anger against ourselves.

Miller (1983: 106) adds that, "The greatest cruelty that can be inflicted on children is to refuse to let them express their anger and suffering except at the risk of losing their parents' love and affection." Many children who grow up in dysfunctional families are systematically taught to inhibit and repress their angry, sad and hurt feelings. Frequently we were talked out of our feelings and taught to distrust what we feel and to trust only what others tell us we are feeling.

If you grew up in a dysfunctional family, you probably didn't get your emotional needs met. As a result, it is likely that you experienced many painful feelings during childhood. To make matters worse, no one was there to listen to your feelings, to support you and to nurture, accept and respect you, forcing you to deal with these painful feelings by yourself. In order to deal with this emotional pain by yourself, you began to build defenses against feeling the feelings, trying to shut them out of your awareness. It is likely that this helped you to survive childhood, but, as a result, you may have become totally out of touch with your true feelings. Without awareness of your true feelings, you lose the fullness and richness of life.

Co-dependent Ways to Handle Feelings

- Cry when you need to get angry.
- Get angry to cover up your fear, sadness or hurt.
- Get depressed instead of taking action.
- Act strong and block out your feelings.
- Blame your feelings on others. ("You made me mad.")
- Believe that the expression of certain feelings is a sign of weakness. (Men don't cry, women shouldn't get angry.)
- Let the feelings of others control your thoughts, feelings and actions.
- Let your thoughts block feelings or feelings block thoughts.
- Only express justified or "racket" feelings, trying to control others.
- Give more power to your feelings than they deserve. ("If I started crying, I would never be able to stop," or "If I got angry, I would hurt someone.")
- Believe feelings are bad and should be avoided. Become addicted to a substance or activity to avoid feeling anything.

Healthy Ways to Handle Feelings

- When you feel angry, or scared or mad, say so and ask for what you want from others.

- Use your feelings to help you make decisions.

- Identify each separate feeling and don't use one to block another.

- Own your feelings and take responsibility for being the source of your feelings.

- Realize that you can think and feel at the same time, and then do it.

- Recognize your "racket" feelings and don't use them to manipulate others.

- Stay current in the expression of your feelings and don't store them up.

- Embrace your feelings as your friends and allies instead of as enemies to be avoided.

- Allow yourself to experience your feelings as fully as possible when they surface.

- Remember that there are no "bad feelings" and that there is an important purpose for each feeling.

TOOLS FOR LEARNING TO FEEL AGAIN

Tools for Working Alone

- Develop a feeling journal for yourself. Make a list of feelings you felt during the day. Enter in your journal when you felt each feeling, where you felt the feeling and any expression of the feeling if there was an expression. If you wish, you may record only those times you felt or were aware of a feeling but experienced or remember no expression of that feeling. Chart your progress over time. Notice what feelings you can identify but can't express. Notice if certain feelings are missing from your list.

- Take inventory of the kinds of feelings that were expressed in your family of origin by your mother, your father and your siblings. Whose pattern do you most often follow?

• Make a list of the things that happened to you as a child about which you could have been angry, sad, scared, happy or excited. Next to each entry, place an (E) if you expressed the feelings of anger, sadness, fear, happiness or excitement. Notice in which situations you repressed or held back your feelings. Finally compare your two lists to see if you are still responding the way you did as a child or if you have changed your feeling response patterns.

Tools for Therapy

A good therapist can provide the same kind of support for your basic needs that can be provided by a cooperative partner. The main difference is that your therapist may be more skilled in helping you reconnect with your deepest feelings and providing an opportunity for you to express them in a safe, supportive environment.

• Breath work is a powerful therapy tool that can enable you to regain contact with your deep hurt or sadness. Old patterns can lock into your body, and breath work can help you connect with and release many old feelings. The breathing technique we use is a connected breathing pattern. You "pull" on inhalation and let go on exhalation. Connect both inhale and exhale so there is no pause between them. Visualize a circle, with the inhale as one half of the circle and the exhale as the other half. As repressed material begins to loosen, all you have to do is keep breathing. You may experience shaking or tingling in your arms and legs and a sense of release of tension in your stomach or chest. About 45 minutes to 1 1/2 hours of this kind of breath work can cause many old patterns locked in your body to release. You may experience an emotional release as well. Following your session, you will feel very relaxed and open. This may be repeated as often as necessary.

Tools for Support Groups

• Support groups can be helpful in giving support to your feelings. One important way groups can support your feelings is through feedback. An exercise that is useful for this is called "strength bombardment." Each person is given two minutes to tell the group his or her major strengths and resources. Then the group has three minutes to tell the person what strengths they see in him or her. Groups no larger than six people work best.

Tools for Partnerships

A lot of healing for co-dependents is at the feeling level. Usually it involves being in a relationship where you can finally get your basic needs met. What you probably need most from your partner is:

- to have them show understanding and respect for your needs and feelings
- to have them listen to your feelings and take them seriously
- to have them provide mirroring so you can see who you really are
- to be able to learn from them and them from you.

These qualities are expressed in many ways in an intimate relationship and are the very thing that can provide the support for you to complete your psychological birth.

• Each person thinks of a current relationship conflict they have with each other. Take turns first blaming everything that happened on your partner, then blaming everything that happened on yourself and then finally looking at what was your "responsibility" in the situation and how each of you may not have acted with the full response-ability. Ask yourself, "What other responses did I have the ability to make but didn't?"

Case Example

Cynthia first came to me (Janae) for therapy requesting help with sexual problems in her relationship with Don. She had first stopped enjoying sex and finally had stopped having sex. Don was upset and insisted that she get counseling.

It was obvious from Cynthia's first few words that she was severely impaired in her feelings and totally fused with Don. Her complete focus was on "getting well" so Don could have sex with her. Cynthia reminded me of a wind-up doll as she talked. Her body movements were rigid and jerky. Her eyes were somewhat vacant and looked into the distance. Her voice was a monotone with virtually no feeling quality. She could have been relating a story about some distant acquaintance, as there were no feelings—only facts.

Therapy with Cynthia was slow and methodical. First, she had to learn what the common feelings are. Then she had to learn to identify them in herself. This took several months of intensive journaling, participation in a support group and discussions with me. Once she had learned to identify feelings, we worked on accepting them.

Cynthia was prone to unexplained episodes of crying. Don was very uncomfortable with these outbursts, so she had learned to hold the tears until she was alone in the bathroom or driving her car. Cynthia learned to bring her sadness to therapy where I could hold her and comfort her. It took almost eighteen months of intermittent therapy, support group work and working on herself before Cynthia was really okay with her feelings. At that point it became safe to take her feelings into her relationship with Don, and they began working together on their feeling issues.

This kind of preparatory work is often necessary before people with severe feeling dysfunctions can begin the process of working on co-dependency issues in a relationship. The recovery of the feeling function is essential to breaking free of the co-dependency trap. If a person doesn't know how or what they are feeling, they usually also don't know what they want or need. They can't be taught how to ask for what they want and need before they really know what they want to ask for.

CHAPTER FIFTEEN

Healing Your Inner Child

By growing up in a dysfunctional family (that is, a family appropriate for a dominator culture), a co-dependent person is forced to give up his or her True Self and adopt a false or co-dependent self that helped them survive. In most dysfunctional families, the adults have so much trouble playing grown-up that they are not available to support or nurture their children most of the time.

Narcissistic Wounds

During the first year to fifteen months, it is impossible to spoil a child. Children need to be noticed, mirrored, taken seriously, held, nurtured, sung to and indulged in all their needs. This is necessary in order to build healthy narcissism or the ability to love oneself. Children whose basic narcissistic needs were met during this stage of development grow up to be the truly giving and unselfish people of the world. They are able to show caring and compassion for others in healthy ways and to find true joy in service to themselves and others.

If your parents' own narcissistic needs were not met when they were children, they would have had a difficult time responding to you in ways that met your needs. Instead, your parents may have unwittingly behaved out of their own unhealed wounds. Parents who suffer this dysfunction often don't take their children's needs seriously. They make fun of their children, they don't allow their children to express their true feelings, and they have trouble respecting their children as separate individuals with free will of their own. As a result, they tease, lie, beat, threaten, isolate, distrust, scorn, coerce, humiliate, and invade their children's personal space. They may use their children as toys or instruments to satisfy their own ego needs; they withhold or withdraw love and may even subject their children to mental or physical torture. The result is that children suffer countless narcissistic wounds. These are wounds that do not easily heal and that can easily be touched and bruised, as an adult, by an insensitive remark or even an unfriendly look.

Adding to the tragedy is the fact that your parents very likely believed that treating you in this way was for your own good. Either they didn't want to spoil you or they wanted to be seen by others as providing good discipline and social training. In either case, they tried to justify their harsh behavior. The implied message is, "If you had any difficulty as a result of our parenting, *it is your fault.*" Something had to be wrong with you. This is the predominant belief of children who grow up in dysfunctional families.

Surprisingly, many of us believed this and accepted the cruelty inflicted on us as "necessary" or our own fault. We figured out ways to adapt to these demands in order to survive. It is important to change these misperceptions of childhood so that you do not pass them on to your children through "for your own good" kinds of parenting. Also, some parents feel it is necessary to do the same thing to their children to prove to themselves that their parents really did love them. It is hard to face the fact that they *didn't* and probably *couldn't* love you as much as you needed. Almost everyone makes a "secret vow" with themselves that, when they grow up, they will not say or do to their children the hurtful things that were said or done to them. Unfortunately, almost everyone, in the stress of playing grown-up, experiences breaking that vow and finds themselves saying and doing to their children exactly what was done to them, often using the same methods and words.

The vicious cycle of cruelty that provides the "glue" for a dominator society will go unchecked from generation to generation if this pattern isn't dealt with. It means reconnecting with your inner child, which is where your true feelings and your True Self are hiding. Your ego defenses were created to protect your inner child from harm. What happens, however, when you hide something like your true feelings or True Self from others is that you end up hiding them from yourself as well. There is an important adage that seems to apply here: "You can't fix something until you know how it got broken."

Again, the most direct way to learn how you got broken in childhood is to reexamine your childhood through an awareness of your co-dependent patterns in the present. These patterns offer you clues to what really happened to you as a child. Even though you can't remember what actually happened to you, you can see and feel what must have happened, as you examine your own co-dependent patterns.

A lot of the work involves re-experiencing your feelings as well. When you experience a painful, hurt feeling (a narcissistic wound), ask yourself to remember times earlier in life when you felt this way. Another important part of the process is to mourn the loss of the connection you once had to your True Self and your Inner Child. An important part of the recovery process is feeling the sadness and grieving these losses.

The table below describes and compares some of the common characteristics of the co-dependent self and the True Self or Inner Child.

COMMON CHARACTERISTICS
OF THE CO-DEPENDENT SELF AND THE TRUE SELF

The Co-dependent Self Is . . .	*The True Self Is . . .*
a false person	a real person
an adapted person	a free person
an artificial person	a genuine person
a planner and plotter	spontaneous
withholding	giving and communicating
closed to feedback	open to feedback
critical, envious, idealized, perfectionistic	accepting of self and others
conforming	compassionate
conditionally loving	unconditionally loving
passive or aggressive	assertive
rational, logical	intuitive
serious	playful
unfeeling	feeling
distrusting	trusting
one who avoids being nurtured	one who enjoys being nurtured
one who controls and withdraws	one who surrenders
self-righteous	self-caring
contracting, fearful	expansive, loving
separated from God and others	connected to God and others

Because our culture still is oriented largely to a dominator model, most of us have learned to hide our True Selves because we are afraid we will be hurt or rejected again. In a dominator culture, the more open you are with your True Self, the more you risk your unhealed narcissistic wounds being exposed, making you feel vulnerable and scared.

As we begin to orient more toward a partnership model, many of us are supporting one another in our attempts to complete our stifled psychological development. Still, it takes considerable spiritual courage to reclaim your True Self and to heal it. But even though it is frightening and you may sometimes get hurt by being more vulnerable, it is worth it because you *feel so much more alive* when you connect with and live out of your True Self and Inner Child.

The Conditions That Stifled the Development of the True Self

There are a number of factors that come from the structure of our dominator culture that may have been present in your family of origin. These conditions led to the stifling of the True Self and the development of the false self or co-dependent self in its place. They are:

- Rigid and compulsive rules

- Perfectionistic, punitive parents

- Rigid and compulsive roles. These roles were prescribed according to the needs of parents. "You are the smart one, she is the pretty one in this family."

- Lots of family secrets

- Addictions to such things as alcohol, drugs, eating, work, sex, another person, etc.

- Serious and burdened atmosphere. Everyone acts like a victim and the only humor is making fun of others and having children or outsiders be the butt of jokes.

- No personal privacy or personal boundaries. Children are given no privacy rights and no personal boundaries.

- One or more parents is chronically ill, either mentally or physically

- Parents with co-dependent relationships

- Physical, sexual or emotional abuse of a child by an adult or adults

- Parents who instilled a false sense of loyalty to the family.

- No one was allowed to talk to outsiders about the family. Resistance to outsiders.

- No strong feelings were permitted by the children

- Conflicts between family members were ignored or denied

- No unity in the family. Some family members join together in subgroups to protect themselves and to abuse other family members.

The Steps in the Progression of Co-dependency

- Inadequate bonding; very little nurturing and care-giving
- Invalidation and repression of all internal cues
- Rewards for pleasing others, no rewards for independent acts
- No support for developing personal boundaries
- Failure to become autonomous, leading to increased dependency on external rewards from others and fear of abandonment
- Increased numbness to internal emotional pain
- Development of compulsive and addictive behaviors to avoid feeling the pain
- Development of shame and guilt, contributing to further loss of self-esteem
- Feeling out of control, leading to manipulative and controlling behaviors
- Development of ego defenses such as projection, denial, rationalizations
- Developing stress-related illnesses
- Increased use of compulsive and addictive acts to control self and others
- Difficulty with intimacy
- Frequent mood swings
- Lying, cheating and other antisocial acts
- Chronic unhappiness
- Life in crisis and breakdown, feelings of death being near

The Healing Process

For you to heal your Inner Child and reconnect with your True Self, you will need to engage in a healing process that involves:

- Discovering and learning to be with your Inner Child more and more each day

- Learning to define your own needs and wants

- Developing effective ways to get your needs and wants met without controlling or manipulating others

- Learning to identify and re-experience your narcissistic wounds and allow yourself to feel the pain and hurt in the presence of people who are safe and supportive

- Learning to identify and work through your core issues or incomplete developmental tasks. You will need to take charge of fixing these "broken" aspects of yourself and learn to integrate them into your True Self.

- Creating a support system of like-minded people who are willing to create partnership relationships.

TOOLS FOR HEALING YOUR INNER CHILD

Tools for Working Alone

- Recall your earliest childhood memory or a recurring childhood dream. Write it out in as great a detail as you can, using as many of your senses as possible. Describe what you saw, heard, felt, smelled, tasted or intuited. Then write what you think you concluded about yourself as a result of this experience or dream. An alternative method is to draw a picture of your memory or dream. This allows you to observe the memory or dream more objectively. Usually there is an important lesson, pattern or principle imbedded in the memory or dream that is still trying to happen in your life. You can use this tool to gain more awareness of the issue and then begin to explore ways to resolve it.

I (Barry) remember a client talking about this exercise. She said she remembered sitting on the grass by herself when she was about the age of two. She looked around and no one was there. She remembered feeling scared and lonely and confused and yet she wasn't crying. In the middle of telling about this memory, she suddenly burst into tears with deep sobs. When she stopped crying, she told me that she realized at that early age she had decided to take care of others and not cry. No matter how lonely and scared she was, she was going to be a "good girl" and not force her parents to hear her crying out, and instead would deny her own needs.

· Another powerful tool for healing your Inner Child is mirror work. There are many ways to do this, but it is important to sit or stand in front of a full-length mirror and learn to love yourself. Say to yourself in the mirror, "I love you because you are smart." You may have to look at the resistance you have to loving yourself. This is also a good way to build object constancy and be able to find new ways to see yourself as someone to be loved.

Tools for Therapy

There are many core issues that can be worked on in therapy. The process of therapy can help you become more aware of these issues in your life, help you to explore the issue and, finally, to take some action to correct the issue. One of the most important issues for healing your Inner Child is learning to grieve the loss of your True Self and healing your narcissistic wounds from childhood. Group therapy is particularly useful for this kind of work. Psychodrama and Gestalt Therapy techniques can be very useful to reown your Inner Child. Breath work, guided imagery, art, movement, play therapy and some kinds of body work also can be useful to help you grieve your losses.

· The following is a guided imagery exercise that is designed for a therapy group or a support group. It is best done with soft music and soft lighting. The leader or a designated person needs to read the guided imagery text while others sit or lie on the floor with their eyes closed. This can be a powerful tool and should be followed by some integration activity such as allowing people to talk about their experience.

Inner Child Meditation

Begin by imagining that you are lying on the shore next to a beautiful calm lake . . . (pause) . . . Feel the sun pouring down upon you . . . (pause) . . . Be aware of a gentle breeze sweeping lightly across your body and keeping you cool . . . (pause) . . . Note the smells and the sounds around you . . . (pause) . . . What are you feeling inside? What are you thinking? Now relax your body even more and imagine being filled completely with calmness, filled with the calmness of that lake . . . washing over you, through you and in you . . . What are you feeling now? . . . Now begin to experience this calmness, this lake within you, as a flowing source of love . . . Feel this love filling your whole body, relaxing you completely, opening you to streams of love flowing through you. . . .

Now remember back to a time when you were a child, before the age of ten. Picture yourself now as a child. See this child standing in front of you. Notice what this child is wearing. Look at this child—look into this child's eyes and send love and receive love. . . . Reach out your hands and take hold of the child's hands and begin to dance with the child around and around. Listen to this child laugh and giggle, playing the way that children do. Feel the warmth of meeting this child . . . Hold the child close to you and hug the child like you have never been hugged before. Hug the child like you always wanted your parents to hug you. . . . And kiss the child on the forehead and hold the child around the waist to snuggle up with you. . . . Pull the child into your body— tell the child that you love him or her and that you never want this child to leave you and that you always want to be able to play this way. . . .

Remember that this is your Inner Child whom you never need to leave again. . . . When you are feeling afraid or feeling old or when you feel like no one loves you, join again with your Inner Child and hold him or her like you always wanted to be held. . . . Don't be ashamed to cry a few tears and express your love completely, for that Inner Child is who you really are . . . your innocence—your true self. . . .

This is what you gave up for your false self. . . . Now you can reclaim what you lost long ago. . . . Treasure your true self—love it and hug it and take it with you to the world. . . . Treasure it . . . but more than all of those things, allow your Inner Child to be visible and alive in everything you do. . . .

Tools for Support Groups

• This activity can help you integrate positive, joyful feelings. Each group member writes down as many peak experiences as he or she can think of. Peak experiences are defined as times of great happiness and joy when you are filled with delight. They are the happiest moments of your life. Just write down a few key words like "Time watching sunset on beach with J" for each experience. Divide the group into sub-groups of two or three where each person shares his or her peak experiences. Have them look for patterns of experiences such as "in nature", "with my husband", "with my kids," etc.

• Finally, ask group members to share some ways they think they can introduce more joy into their lives by creating additional opportunities for peak experiences. Each person should design a course of action and share the plan in the small group.

Tools for Partnerships

• Each of us has a two- to three-year-old child within us that never got enough holding, nurturing or being cared for. Working cooperatively, you and your partner can take turns asking to be held, comforted or cared for in some important way. The key to this exercise is that you each ask directly: "Will you hold me and rock me for a while?" In this way many of the old narcissistic wounds can be healed.

• Another way to connect with your Inner Child is through play. Partners who can play together will find much joy in their relationship. Working cooperatively with your partner, select an age below age ten. Decide on some play activity that the two of you can do together. Take turns playing together as children (i.e., swinging on the swings, playing in a sand-box, riding a bicycle together, climbing trees, etc.). This may seem like a silly activity at first, but partners who have done this have found a kind of intimacy together that they cherish.

• Each of you take a large sheet of paper and make a list of all the things your parents, teachers, friends or other adults said were wrong with you as a child. List as many as you can think of. When you are done, look at who the message came from originally. Finally, sit facing your partner and read each one of these messages to him or her, asking him/her to speak directly to your Inner Child saying, "That is not true of you. I see you as (*positive mirroring*)." Take turns reading your lists to each other and getting support for your Inner Child.

Case Example

This case example relates to my (Barry's) own work on a re-curring childhood dream that helped me reconnect with my Inner Child. The dream, which occurred many times during childhood and once or twice since then, is as follows:

> I am being chased by some monster. I run out of my bedroom and down the upstairs hallway of the house where I grew up. The monster is gaining on me and I can't run fast enough to get away. I can feel the hot breath of the monster on my neck and he is about to grab me when I turn the corner in the hall and am at the top of the stairs. The only way I can

get away from the monster is to leap from the top step. Instead of falling, I fly or float down to the bottom of the stairs. I land on my feet safely and then I wake up.

I never did anything with that dream until several years ago when I became curious about its meaning. The first thing I did was to pick out some of the key words and then speculate on what they might mean. The key words or phrases for me were "monster, can't run, hot breath, grab me, turn the corner, leap, falling, fly or float, land on my feet and wake up." Then I identified or located each word or phrase in a part of my body. Following were words of meaning for the key words: "me, my mother, animal, kill, too slow, etc.—(all in one sentence). The following body parts came to mind: "legs, neck, hands, etc.— (all in one sentence).

Key Words	Meaning of Key Words	Body Part
monster	me, my mother, animal, kill	legs
can't run	too slow to catch on, toilet training, crippled	neck
hot breath	red, passion, fear, dog	hands
grab me	never, why me, serious	buttocks
turn corner	car, new beginning	eyes
leap	fear, look before you leap	face
falling	sinking, say good-bye, fatal boat, rocket	arms
land on feet	charmed life, smelling like roses, blessed	feet
wake up	call, message, awareness	ears

The next thing I did with the dream was to act it out in slow motion. At one point, as I am running away from the monster, my left foot and left ankle start to weaken and I almost stumble, but I maintain my balance. Then I asked myself, "What would have happened if I fell down?" The answer came almost immediately, "You would have to face your monster!" I thought, "What would happen now if I turned to face my monster instead of running away?" This was an important shift for me. I saw that as a child I could only run away, but now I am no longer a child and I don't have to be afraid to face my monster. In fact, facing my monster may have a lot to do with reclaiming my Inner Child.

So I decided to turn and face my monster and draw a picture of the monster. It was a half-human, half-animal-looking thing. It had on a black hood like an executioner, with pointed teeth and deep-set red eyes, and not at all friendly looking.

I decided then to dialogue with the monster and here is what I found out. I asked him who he is and he replied, "The executioner. The one who is going to chop off your head. You have been tried, found guilty and sentenced to death by being beheaded."

Then I asked him, "What was my crime?" He said,

> Being born. You came along at the wrong time. No one was ready for you. They thought they were ready for you, but when you came along they found out all too quickly that you were too much trouble. So they sent me to chase you away and make you so scared that you wouldn't cause them any problems. They were hoping you would grow up fast before everyone found out how inadequate they were for the job of raising you. You should have known better than to come into this family and upset the apple cart. You used poor judgment. Poor timing. Any other time would have been better. It was the worst possible time.

I worked on this dream some more by making a clay image of the monster's face. Then I painted my own face and became the monster during a therapy group. I also realized that the part of me that ran away and leaped to safety was the part that was trying to escape my parents' control, as well as my own need to take care of or please others. In the dream I actually leaped to safety. From this I learned I can be free of my false self if I take the risk. This led me to remember all the risks I had taken in my life and how I always landed on my feet. I began to see the dream in a new light. There is a part of me that wants to be free and actually knows how to get free if it is challenged to do so by a monster or a part that wants to control me or chop off my head. This part is really my Inner Child. He is so free he can do magical things like fly and always land on his feet. I keep the clay image of my monster on the nightstand next to my bed as a reminder of the role this important ally plays in the reconnection to my Inner Child.

This example illustrates that the desire to reconnect with our Inner Child is with us constantly. If we don't pay attention to the urgings of this incomplete process, it will press for completion through our dreams as well as any other means available. It seems like a paradox, but it is through this reconnection with our Inner Child that we finally can grow up and enjoy life more fully. Otherwise, we are stuck with "playing" grown-up, and we all know that truly is *serious business*.

CHAPTER SIXTEEN

Building Your Boundaries

Symbiotic Families

Parents who have not experienced their own psychological birth will inadvertently create a symbiotic or enmeshed system in which each member of the family has to become co-dependent with every other member of the family. What results is a spiderweb-like structure that restrains everyone and keeps them enmeshed with each other. This kind of symbiotic family system fosters beliefs, values, judgments and myths that support the structure and provides an apparent united front to present to the world. Rebellion and other attempts to become independent from the system are usually countered with shame, humiliation, physical abuse, withdrawal of love and threats of abandonment. The system is reinforced by promises of oneness and security; with pride, egotism and superficial attention or approval.

Family members often describe this symbiosis as an overwhelming experience of suffocation and loss of individual identity. There usually is no space for separateness in this kind of system. Everything the members do is designed to help perpetuate the family system. The system is not set up to support or perpetuate individuality. This phenomenon is sometimes known as the co-dependent family. The co-dependent family functions much the same as the co-dependent stage of relationship in which there is enmeshment of feelings, problems, thoughts, dreams and needs, except that it involves more than two people. Each person's individual psychology is present in a co-dependent family, but he or she is unable to identify with it or to claim it.

THE CO-DEPENDENT FAMILY

Symbiosis in families may be difficult to recognize as a serious problem because it supports the "We're one, big happy family" fantasy that once was considered a healthy form of relationship. Once we understand the important need for experiencing our psychological birth and becoming a separate person, symbiosis can be seen more clearly as a dysfunctional form of relationship.

Symbiosis may be expressed in such things as expectations that a son be called "Junior" or follow the family tradition of being a doctor or athlete. Other legacy issues such as living close to home, having a certain number of children or marrying a particular kind of mate are really subtle forms of symbiosis. These kinds of life decisions are not negative in *themselves*. It is the *absence of conscious personal choice* for the individual in these matters and the many external *expectations* that are the issue, for these kinds of limitations inhibit the unfoldment of the True Self. Symbiotic dynamics also are usually unconscious, which means that the people involved have little awareness that they are following someone else's expectations.

Stories of parents who drive their children to perform as exceptional students or athletes illustrate the unhealthy need of the adults to be validated through their children. Children who are subjected to parents with exaggerated needs for fame and glory often become empty, driven adults themselves and feel they have never achieved quite enough. In spite of their achievements, they frequently suffer from low self-esteem and poor self-concept and experience themselves as failures.

Typically, it is a feeling of suffocation that motivates an individual to get out of this enmeshment. They may feel as though they are dying or experience some illness or physical ailment that activates their death fear. It is only then that they dare to try to leave the system.

Daring to be Different From Your Co-dependent Family

When you make the decision to change yourself and your life, you are in effect deciding to leave the collective mind and be different. This process, which Carl Jung called "individuation," is really a task of separating yourself from the chaos and confusion of your family, especially from your parents.

This may seem like a perfectly logical and appropriate thing to do. Your family, however, may be unhappy with you. They may even be upset, hurt or angry with you. When you decide to be separate, you will disturb the delicate structure of the family spiderweb and may cause it to collapse. This will trigger everyone's fears so that they will try to stop you. You may find them using the old enforcement tools (shame, withdrawal of love, etc.) even more to keep you in your place. They may try to convince you that you're crazy or sick or even try to hospitalize you. They will definitely not let go of you easily, especially if you have been a key figure in playing out the family drama.

Outside support at this point is often critical, for you may indeed begin to doubt your own sanity. Friends, therapists and group members are invaluable as allies who can help you deal with the family's parting shots. People who have not built an external support system prior to leaving find getting out much more difficult.

Who Owns the Problem

One of the ways that systems keep members enmeshed is through group ownership of all problems. When father loses his glasses, everyone must hunt for them. If Suzy comes home with a poor report card, everyone monitors her homework after school. This keeps the whole system in chaos and confusion and prevents the development of individuality. This kind of behavior is a group rescue that prevents individual members from being responsible and receiving the consequences of their own actions. For example, if father had to attend an important meeting without his glasses as a consequence of misplacing them, he might learn to keep track of them.

There are three categories of ownership that help you distinguish between what is yours and what is not yours. They help determine responsibility (response-ability). These categories help you determine what is—

- Mine (I'm going somewhere and I lost my car keys.)

- Yours/Theirs (You/They are going somewhere and you/they lost the car keys.)

- Ours (We are going somewhere and the car keys are lost.)

Each of these categories requires a different response:

- Mine—I am responsible and I need to respond.

- Yours/Theirs—You/They are responsible. I will listen reflectively, offer support if asked, and allow you/them to respond.

- Ours—We both are responsible and we both need to respond.

Fuzziness about ownership originates in infancy when the child isn't able to respond very well, so the mother, father and siblings do the responding. This pattern of responding turns into rescuing when the child becomes old enough to be responsible. This prolonged care reinforces passivity.

Boundaries

The task of becoming separate and autonomous means you will be able to separate yourself from others and create individual boundaries that help you form an identity of your own.

INDIVIDUATED FAMILY

Individual boundaries include your own body, your feelings, thoughts, ideas, needs, beliefs and wants. Having boundaries creates a whole new set of rules about how people interact with each other. These rules include:

- People need to ask permission before they can cross over each other's personal and psychological boundary lines.
- Response-ability is assigned by ownership of the problem.
- People do not "own" or "belong" to each other.

In symbiotic families, there are virtually no personal boundaries between family members. In more co-dependent families where the parents are severely symbiotic, the adults and children may even reverse roles. This is very common in alcoholic homes where the children may shop, clean and put the drunken parent(s) to bed. The adults may also turn to the children for the nurturing, love, affection and comfort that parents would ordinarily give rather than receive. This creates an atmosphere in which incest or sexual abuse is highly likely, which is why it is quite prevalent in alcoholic families.

Incest and Sexual Abuse

Fathers who become involved in incest with their children are almost always very symbiotic. Their insufficient bonding and an inability to separate create strong needs for warmth, closeness, acceptance and intimacy. A father who has not experienced this is usually unable to even verbalize these needs. He will just yearn for someone to be close to and to be held and touched. Strong fears of abandonment make fulfilling these needs with an adult woman too risky and too scary. The warmth and innocence of the child, however, soothes these fears and creates the safety necessary for their unmet narcissistic needs to surface. Such men are literally thrown back into an infantile state in which their own needs and feelings are regarded as most important. The false belief that children can't remember anything until they were five or six years old supports a "doll fantasy" form of relationship. The following poem written by a thirty-year-old woman describes her relationship with her alcoholic father.

THIS DOLL IS A CHILD

Pretty little girl
Dressed in a frilly dress.   Hair fixed nice
A doll to play with

Some
Combed her hair   Made her clothes   Tied her shoes

Others
Gave her baths   Helped her in the bathroom
. . . and rubbed 'till it hurt   with perverse explorations.

Wonderful doll she was

Do what she was asked   Help along the way
She'd keep him company on a laundry day,
Never making a sound as he would play
Then cast her aside until time to play again.

She'd keep him company while Mom was away.

No one ever considered

What he did with his toy doll   Too busy to play other games

Cast her aside
put her on the shelf
Until he wanted to play again

He knew she'd be there.

This special doll has feelings
SHE DOES NOT LIKE
Sitting on the shelf   His kind of play   Thrown on the floor
when through
She fears his anger

Her brilliant eyes shine
From tears   Not happiness
like they should
She becomes more quiet
Realizing she is only a playtoy
who cannot act on her own

She HURTS

This Doll is a child!
To be
Guided   Loved   Nurtured   Helped

Not for
Sordid pleasure
To be tossed aside
She is not a possession
She is not a toy
How will she ever grow up this way?

Symbiotic fathers often do not know how to be close and affectionate in a non-sexual way, to meet their own needs to
belong or to have a warm relationship in a non-physical way.
They sexualize most of their relationships. When a symbiotic
father turns to his daughter for sex in an attempt to meet his
symbiotic needs, he is seldom aware of what he really needs.
Most men who commit incest are completely out of touch with

their needs and have no experience in meeting them in healthy ways.

Sexual abuse, whether it be between a mother and child, father and child, brother and sister or teacher and student, can be traced back to the dominator model of society. The hierarchical ranking of one individual or group over another sets up inequities of power in which the higher-ranked group has "permission" to persecute and victimize another.

From this perspective, incest and sexual abuse can be viewed as problems related both to co-dependency and incomplete developmental issues and to a dysfunctional social structure. This view helps support the symbiotic, perpetrating parent or adult as someone who needs treatment and understanding rather than being treated as a criminal. There *are* adults who are psychopathic, who had almost no bonding or care as an infant and who are out to get revenge on everyone. The circumstances that trigger their incestuous acts are different than for the symbiotic parent or adult. The psychopathic parent is not included in this discussion of incest and sexual abuse. Looking at incest and sexual abuse from a developmental and cultural perspective, it becomes clear that society needs to examine them as issues of the larger community.

A Cultural Epidemic

Newspapers, magazines and books are full of information about the rising incidence of incest and sexual abuse. It is quite obvious that these problems are not isolated to families, as the incidents involve teachers, principals, ministers, priests, coaches, day-care operators and scout leaders. While symbiosis helps to explain the motives behind incest and sexual abuse, does it explain the increasing number of sexual incidents and attacks that are reported?

There are several factors that help explain the epidemic. First is the increasing amount of awareness children have that incest or sexual abuse is inappropriate. Many schools and groups have had speakers come with anatomically correct dolls to discuss boundary issues and appropriate versus inappropriate touching. Such discussions frequently reveal that there are victims in the group. The education of children has increased dramatically and so has the reporting system.

Second is the education of adults. Most adults are horrified to discuss the prevalence of sexual abuse and incest. Many educators and health care professionals are receiving training in the identification of child abuse, including sexual abuse. In most states these professionals are now legally compelled to report *suspected* cases of abuse. The penalty clause has convinced many of them to be very conscientious in their reporting. Thus many more cases are now being reported.

A third factor is that there is more support in the legal system for dealing with perpetrators and for supporting victims. Child advocates for victims are more common as are mandatory treatment programs for the perpetrators. This has happened because of the growing awareness that this is like the tip of the iceberg. It cuts across ethnic, social, educational and economic groups. No longer can offenders just be tossed in jail.

The fourth factor is more subtle and is connected to the currents of cultural change. History records measurable shifts back and forth between dominator and partnership trends in societies, even though the dominator model has been the prevailing trend. The records reveal that shifts toward the more feminine values of the partnership model have been followed by a period of resurging masculine values. The period of rising feminine values, such as the Elizabethan age in England and the European Renaissance, are characterized by humanitarianism, creativity, social reforms and greater freedom for women. These have been followed by periods of rising masculine values characterized by renewed attempts to restrict roles (including sexual ones) for women, hostility toward women, aggression, persecution of minorities and authoritarianism.

A more recent major conflict between rising feminine values and the values of the masculine came during the 1800s when the feminist movement was met with an increase in what can now be termed *aggravated assault*: severe, bone-breaking, domestic beatings; setting of a wife on fire; and the putting out of women's eyes. This repeats patterns of witch hunting and burning during the 1300-1400s and again in the late 1600s and early 1700s.

The rise of the feminine in the 1960s and 1970s in the women's liberation movement, the human rights movement and the self-help movement is being countered with a rise in Klu Klux Klan activities, facism, extremist religions, domestic violence, rape, incest and sexual abuse. It is estimated that such crimes now occur in the United States at the rate of one every thirteen seconds. (Jacobs 1984)

During the 1960s, reported rapes in the U.S. increased by over 95%. (Jacobs 1984:5) Even with the increase in reporting, there is still an exceptional rise in statistics. More contemporary acts against women include public executions in Iran for unbecoming conduct and the requirement to wear the veil for women in many Islamic countries.

Another facet of the repression of the feminine has been seen in the abuse directed toward planet Earth. In the last forty years, we have witnessed the planting of missiles and exploding of bombs in Mother Earth's body; the pollution of the air, water and land with toxic chemicals; the stripping of coal and minerals from the Earth's surface; and the mining and casual consumption of Earth's vital elements. These facts portray a disregard for the Earth, sometimes known as Gaia, as a living, feminine being. This disregard is as pervasive as the current disregard for the value of women and feminine perspectives. They must be considered as related phenomenon.

Thoughts About Boundaries

Recognizing and creating personal boundaries are major steps in the healing of co-dependency, for it requires a restructuring of all relationships. One person, whether in a relationship or in a family of ten, arrives at this awareness before others do, frequently creating a crisis. A partner or child who enjoys the symbiotic dynamics (e.g., having all their personal needs cared for when they are capable of taking care of themselves) may be quite upset at this change. They may try to make you feel like a bad person and play on your guilt.

Choosing to create personal boundaries may cause relationships to crumble. Such choices need to be made with forethought and clarity so that you can move through the resistance that you will meet from those who do not want you to change and who resist change themselves. Once you decide to create personal boundaries, it is difficult to turn back. You need to think through the scenarios that may unfold and be prepared to meet them. You also will need the support of others who recognize your need for boundaries and will be there for you when the conflict arises.

TOOLS FOR BUILDING YOUR BOUNDARIES

Tools for Working Alone

• Keep a log in your journal of each time you are aware that someone invades you without your permission. Include such things as allowing inappropriate touching; having sentences cut off or completed for you; people entering private areas such as your bathroom, your desk or your journal. Record also your feelings when they happened and how you responded. Notice the patterns of frequency and your responses. Make agreements with family members regarding your boundaries.

Tools for Therapy

• List the symbiotic/co-dependent relationships that you are currently involved in, along with reasons for and against separating yourself from them. Discuss these with your therapist. Then role play with your therapist ways to break the symbiosis. This is often necessary to help you learn new responses to attempts to keep you attached symbiotically.

Tools for Support Groups

- Create a telephone call system and a list of "retreat houses" for your group members so that any member can find quick support if they need it during a crisis when they are trying to break free of a co-dependent system.

- Develop at least two friends who will help you remember in your weak moments exactly how bad your symbiotic/co-dependent relationship(s) is/are so that you can call them and ask for a reminder.

- Seek out groups of people who are living their lives as you'd like to, so you can use them as models to help you develop your new self in a supportive environment.

Tools for Partnerships

- Contract with each other to provide feedback about behavior that invades each other's personal space (finishing sentences, reading mail, rearranging personal belongings).

- Individually read this checklist and check questions you can respond to with "yes." Then share the results.

  - Do you have a sense of being "crazy"?
  - Do you have large periods of memory loss about your childhood?
  - Are you more than 50 lbs. overweight?
  - Have you been abused or abused someone else?
  - Does sex turn you off?
  - Do you have trouble maintaining an intimate relationship?
  - Are you ashamed of your body?
  - Do you sexualize relationships even if you don't want to?
  - Do you regularly experience migraines, gastro-intestinal disturbances or genitourinary disturbances?
  - Do you have a general sense of depression that you can't shake?

– Do you "freeze" in certain situations such as when you
encounter an authority figure?
– Are you afraid of having children or being around them?
– Are you accident-prone?

If you answer "yes" to two or more of these questions, you
may have incest in your past and not remember it. Sometimes
memories of incest are buried for thirty or forty years before
they surface.

Case Example

Joyce seemed like a model client: aged forty-one with no major
problems, good self-awareness and just interested in growth
and a better relationship with her husband. Slowly a different
pattern began to emerge. She had no memory of her childhood
below age ten, and a previous history of being battered, accident-
prone, having problems with authority figures, being turned
off by sex and having chronic gastro-intestinal problems. We
recognized these symptoms as a good indication of sexual abuse
during childhood, possibly incest. While Joyce had no memory
of any kind of abuse, she also had no memories before age ten.

Gradually her childhood memories started to return, and
Joyce began to recall incidents from about age four that involved
an uncle. She couldn't believe it because her uncle was highly
respected by her family. Her father died in the war when she
was three and her uncle (his brother) helped to support the
family and saved the family from having to split apart. Her
mother told her how grateful Joyce should be because without
him Joyce would have had to go away to an orphanage. For
almost a year, she found it difficult to validate her faint memories. She began to believe she must have made up the whole
thing. Joyce tried hypnosis but even that didn't help her achieve
memory clarity.

This is a very typical pattern for people who have repressed
the memory of sexual abuse since early childhood. There is no
one to substantiate the faint memory and the general feelings.
Friends often discourage making a fuss about something that

might have happened almost forty years ago. The truth lies somewhere in Joyce's memory and in her body memory. Her physical symptoms were too obvious.

Joyce's breakthrough came through a series of events, some happening in therapy and some outside. We asked her to talk to several other adult survivors of incest who remembered the abuse after many years. This was very helpful because it validated some of Joyce's feelings and sensations in her body.

The other breakthrough came shortly after that in a group setting where Joyce reported her conversations with other adult survivors. She talked about associating a vomiting sensation in her stomach with her memories, and as she did that she clutched her midsection. We asked her to draw the sensation on paper. As she drew a red and black circular image on the paper, her face became ashen. She said, "Oh my God, I remember him forcing his penis into my mouth. I started choking and I almost vomited. It was my uncle; I saw his face."

It took Joyce almost two years more to get to the other side of the problem. She continued working hard in therapy to accept the guilt and the shame. One evening she tearfully recalled how much she needed and enjoyed the attention her uncle gave her. He took her with him on trips and when he didn't, he always brought her a present. He had money, position and prestige in her family, so she gained some of that by being his favorite niece. He threatened to have her sent away to an orphanage if she ever told anyone. She said she got used to his sexual advances. Most of all she needed his attention.

It was important for Joyce to admit how much she enjoyed her uncle's attention and affection and to acknowledge the desperate need she had to receive love. This helped her to heal her wounds and make a shift. For most adult survivors of incest or sexual abuse, this is the hardest part to accept: to admit and accept the fact that they may have enjoyed the bonding part of the relationship even though the sexual part was repulsive. When adult survivors can make this distinction and separate the two parts of the relationship, it becomes easier for them to feel all of their feelings and move through the last stage of recovery.

CHAPTER SEVENTEEN

Forming Bonds of Intimacy

BONDING: A CRITICAL REQUIREMENT

In Chapter Four, you learned about bonding and how critical it is in helping a child experience the safety and security of a total connection with his or her mother. You also learned the importance of the father/child bonding in the eventual resolution of the issues of counter-dependency. This chapter will focus on other kinds of bonding problems, as well as how to repair these weak strands of connection.

Information about the importance of good bonding has increased in volume dramatically during the past twenty years. Information has been drawn together from different groups studying human behavior and development, such as educational psychologists, clinical psychologists, mental health professionals, prenatal and perinatal medical specialists, teachers and parents. Out of the information and research is coming consistent confirmation of the significance of bonding. The lack of good infant bonding is now recognized as a critical factor in creating learning disorders, co-dependency, autism in children, antisocial personality disorders, feeling disorders, borderline personality disorders, dysfunctional family relationships and perhaps in larger cultural problems such as global environmental issues. The evidence is overwhelming. Poorly bonded people have trouble living functional lives.

The Elements of Bonding

Joseph Chilton Pearce (1977, 1985) focused on bonding as a central issue of early childhood development, looking at the circumstances that prevent it as well as the effects of bonding, or a lack of it, on learning and relating. He identifies five different steps/elements in creating good bonding in the mother/ child relationship during the first few hours, days and months:

- holding the child and also molding it to the mother and the father (skin-to-skin contact is best)
- prolonged and steady eye contact with the child
- smiling at the child
- making soothing sounds, especially singing to the child
- body stimulation such as stroking and massaging the child.

Pearce (1985) also identifies eight developmental stages of bonding, seeing human development as a series of bondings that hold together the process of life. He describes it as an instinct that carries humans toward the full development of spiritual capacities. His developmental stages of bonding are:

1. with the mother (at birth and immediately after)
2. with the father and family (immediately after birth)
3. with the Earth (about age four)
4. with society (about age seven)
5. with society's body of knowledge (age eleven)

6. with a person of the opposite sex (after puberty)

7. with offspring (as a parent)

8. spiritual bonding.

The first seven stages together comprise an eighth step that Pearce calls "spiritual bonding" and, if this is completed, a person becomes capable of feeling connected to the whole world and everything in it.

As with any developmental process, it is possible to return to points where the process broke down and repair the brokenness. The breakdown of the early childhood bonding can be healed through committed relationships, therapy, support groups and individual work. The breakdown of the bonding with the Earth can also be repaired, but we know less about it. Retreats to nature, combined with practices from Native American traditions, as well as gardening and planting trees and flowers, are more common ways. There is still a lot to learn about completing this form of bonding and developing partnership with the Earth.

The incomplete bonding with society is, we believe, being expressed in the movement toward "community." The 12-step programs, which began with Alcoholics Anonymous, have been described by M. Scott Peck (1987) as the best examples of true community in this country. In community, according to Peck, group members are able to be their True Selves and find support for healing their wounds. Many religious and spiritual groups, as well as some people in business, are developing practices within their organizations to bring people closer so that they can work and live more in partnership. Some corporations are actually bringing the principles and traditions of 12-step programs into their workplace and using them to help create a cooperative corporate culture.

The bonding process builds on each of the previous stages. The degree to which the previous stages are completed determines how well the next stages will get completed. The more bonded a child is to the parents, the more likely he or she is to reach the rich, full existence often referred to as spirituality.

Bonding with society's body of knowledge is both an educational issue and a developmental issue, and it is important to recognize that the effectiveness of our educational system must be examined from both perspectives.

As a developmental issue, it is clear that the degree to which a child has bonded to the mother/father/family determines the degree to which she or he can bond to the Earth and then to society. These stages of bonding then determine how completely he or she will bond with society's body of knowledge— to the concepts, ideas and perceptions about how the world works.

As an educational issue, most schools are structured so that they support co-dependency, actually preventing the completion of these developmental issues. This can further complicate the child's inner trauma, deepening and extending the pattern of co-dependency.

Healthy bonding in schools is supported by activities that are cooperative, recognize individual uniqueness and promote appropriate body contact such as hugging, making "puppy piles" (where everyone lies huddled together on the floor like puppies in a litter), forming arm-to-arm circles for dancing or moving a line of students into a tightly coiled spiral shape. These kinds of activities need to be undergirded with information and considerations on what constitutes appropriate and inappropriate touching, along with firm support in setting individual limits and boundaries about being touched or being in close body contact. Teachers need to talk about these things openly and also model the kind of appropriate behavior that is desired. These kinds of behaviors and a supportive atmosphere set by the classroom teacher will help children learn to discriminate between the healthy characteristics of bonding (which encourage individual needs and boundaries) and the unhealthy characteristics of symbiosis (which inhibit free choice and carry external expectations and deny boundaries and limits).

Bonding with someone of the opposite sex is often inhibited by incomplete bonding during the previous stages, especially those related to societal bonding. Institutions often discourage appropriate opposite sex contact, primarily because it may activate sexual issues. What often happens instead is the creation of co-dependent patterns of dominance and submission where sex is used as a weapon of intimidation and control to reinforce the dominator model. Male/female competition and ranking, not bonding and cooperation, are the norm. If people do not learn male/female bonding skills at home, they certainly won't learn them in institutions.

That means there is a shortage of skills and information to help with parenting offspring. Most parents bumble their way through child-rearing, doing what they can with what they have. Most fathers have no training at all.

In our current stage of the evolutionary process, there is little opportunity for many people to reach the last stage, spirituality. Some do, of course, but it is not because our still largely dominator culture or any of its systems supports it. A few courageous people, with some strong inner drive and a vision of something better, refuse to let the system hold them back. They strive onward in spite of the cultural restrictions and their own wounds. Such people are sometimes called "pathfinders." (Sheehy 1981)

Bonding and Learning

In Chapter Four we stated that poorly bonded or attached children are often afraid of the world and fear change. Their exploring and risk-taking skills are weak and they need constant reinforcement from external sources. Attached children often become rigid, have closed-off feelings and develop compulsive behaviors. Such shortcomings directly interfere with real learning, which involves the use of the sensing, observing, thinking and feeling functions. Real learning requires the child to have self-reflective abilities, full access to his or her feelings, the ability to involve his or her body in the learning process *and* to be able to think.

Attached children can adapt to learning structures that use only the thinking function (which our current dominator-based educational system does). Thinking, especially left-hemispheric thinking (which our current educational system also encourages), supports the dysfunctional behaviors of the attached child. Compartmentalization, reductionism, linear thinking, hierarchical ranking and rationality, all functions of the left hemisphere, dominate Western education.

There are numerous other ways in which educational systems discourage or prevent bonding and the completion of developmental processes. These ways, of course, can be traced directly to the dominator model. Some of these ways include the following:

- They rank members hierarchically, with students and their needs at the very bottom.

- They teach children to adapt to the system by punishing spontaneity and restricting freedoms.

- They assume all responsibility for structuring and evaluating the child's educational experience, discouraging feedback from students.

- They reinforce dependence, symbiosis and isolation.

- They support the system by force or the threat of force, using compulsory attendance requirements and expulsion (withdrawal of "love"), and by requiring degrees and credentials in order to be accepted in the system.

- They teach students to compete rather than cooperate with each other through the use of a competitive grading system.

- They prohibit feelings, personal issues and social interaction in the classroom, stressing only academics.

- They encourage rigid sex roles.

- They devalue diversity and discovery, and value conformity and passivity.

You can see how difficult it is for a human being to reach the stages of male/female bonding and spirituality. The cultural conspiracy, unconscious as it may be, makes interdependency and the fullness it brings almost impossible.

Bonding and Psychopaths

Recent studies (Magid and McKelvey 1988) cite poor bonding between birth and age two as the primary cause of the antisocial personality disorder (APD). People with this disorder (about 15% of this country's adult population) possess a poisonous mix of traits. They are arrogant, shameless, immoral, impulsive, antisocial, superficial, charming, callous, irresponsible, irreverent, cunning and deceitful. They probably won't kill but will lie, cheat and steal readily and feel no guilt. Some extreme examples, such as Charles Manson, are found in jails and mental institutions, but others with less severe symptoms can be found in the mainstream of society and in all walks of life.

The research shows that there are more APD's entering society than ever before. The increase in poor bonding that helps create APD's is attributed to a number of cultural trends:

- the increase in teen pregnancy
- an increase in the number of unprepared teen mothers keeping their babies and parenting them
- rising divorce rates
- increasing child abuse
- more adoptions
- more foster care
- substandard day care

The research also indicates that interruptions in the bonding process such as hospitalization, parental illness and absence significantly disturb the child. This is especially critical at times such as at birth and during the stages of separation between nine months and three years.

Magid and McKelvey identify teenage parenting as the prime cause of the rise of APD's in the United States. Teen mothers are children themselves and do not know how to appropriately interact with their infants. A second important factor in the high rate of APD's is substandard day care. Most day care caregivers are poorly paid and minimally trained. The turnover among them is high and there is often too large a ratio between workers and the children. Substandard day care is a reflection of the low value that our culture places on the development of children.

The treatment of very poorly bonded children who show signs of APD is very difficult. Current treatment focuses on helping the child vent the deep-seated rage and sadness they have repressed over their failure to bond. In "rage-reduction therapy," the child is physically held while being stimulated by the therapist to express their rage and anger. This has proven effective if the child is treated while still young. Once a child reaches the age of sixteen, this treatment doesn't seem to work. These children often go on to jails and social institutions to be "warehoused." This whole phenomenon must be recognized as both a cultural and a developmental issue requiring drastic changes in the way we deal with parenting and the breakdown of the nuclear family. You may be asking yourself, "Where do I turn to heal all this?"

Bonding and Committed Relationships

Drastic changes are already under way inside many individuals, especially those who have recognized their addictive patterns. The crisis of addictions is becoming one of the most common sources of "waking up" experiences. Out of the crises that addictions often bring, people frequently are able to move into recovery programs and begin to restructure themselves and their lives. Through 12-step programs, therapy and work on themselves, people are able to create new beliefs and new behaviors. Once they have done this first step of admitting they have a problem and have broken some of the co-dependent patterns, they often discover the most effective form of therapy available: conscious, committed relationships.

Much of the emerging form of committed relationships might

be termed "reparenting." In reparenting, each partner recognizes the unfinished business with his or her birth parents and willingly works with the other to help him or her heal the wounds and complete the process. When conflict or some other relationship issue brings up old feelings or hurts, your partner can consciously take on the part of a parental figure and provide you with what is missing. Reparenting can include bonding support such as rocking, giving baby bottles, singing, holding and providing touch and skin-to-skin contact. Reparenting can also help people develop the skills necessary for separation by encouraging exploration and risk-taking, by providing reassurance when necessary, by offering positive feedback and affirmative messages at separation successes and by providing mirroring for acts of independence or individuality.

Reparenting is easier when you know what bonding and separation you require. The following exercises will help you find where you have things missing.

TOOLS FOR FORMING BONDS OF INTIMACY

Tools for Working Alone

• In your journal, record interviews with the people who were members of your family during the first two years of your life. If these people are not available to actually interview, then imagine how each person might have responded (both positively and negatively) about your birth into the family. This will help you get a clear picture of what was happening during that period of your life.

• Create methods for supporting your own needs for bonding by finding a doll or teddy bear for comfort. Buy a rocking chair and rock yourself when you feel vulnerable and alone. A music box with nursery tunes is also helpful for comforting yourself.

Tools for Therapy

- Use information, lists and charts from previous exercises and from baby pictures, home movies and talking to your parents to create a composite picture of your first two years of life, focusing on your bonding and separation experiences. Bring this composite picture into therapy to discuss. With your therapist to guide and support you, work to recreate the feelings and experiences of this time period. Try to find your deepest feelings and allow them to surface and be released. If anger comes up, have appropriate props such as bean bags and pillows to beat on. Use an old tennis racquet or plastic baseball bat to hit with. If sadness surfaces, ask your therapist to hold you. Props such as satin-edged blankets, dolls and teddy bears can be helpful with expressing and healing sadness. If you used to suck your thumb, feel free to do that if you need to in your healing. Deep sadness and rage are two of the most difficult feeling states to access, and they almost always require safety and support from a therapist who has done his or her own rage and sadness work.

- Establish a reparenting contract with your therapist. Once you are aware of the incomplete tasks in your early childhood development, you can "contract" with another responsible adult whom you trust to provide some of the missing or inaccurate information you need. You can also use a support group to improve your bonding and help you complete your separation process. Ask your therapist to function as a "contract mother or father" in order to help you fill in the gaps in the parenting you received. Contract parents can provide you with nurturing and information that help correct any misinformation you received as a child, through structured play activities, role playing, reading books to you and any other activities designed to help you complete your incomplete developmental tasks. You may need to temporarily regress to a young age while you are engaged in the process of reparenting. You will need to trust that your contract parent(s) will protect you and comfort you when you feel old feelings such as fear or anger. This kind of deep work is necessary for healing.

Tools for Support Groups

- Create a reparenting group where people can function as a "contract parent" for each other. Also, a support group can help recreate healthy sibling interactions to replace any dysfunctional sibling interactions from childhood.

- To allow this to work most effectively, a three- or four-hour segment of time is needed. You will need to temporarily regress to the age where you believe you want to work and "act that age" throughout the time period. Surprisingly, it is not difficult to remember how to act the age you need to be at because the memories are stored in the nerve endings in your muscles. When you start moving like a two- or three-year-old, your memory of that age is increased. The more you can free yourself to regress to a young age and stay there throughout your contracted time, the more you will gain from this.

- The meeting should start with each person making an explicit contract, asking for what he or she wants or needs and from whom. Half of the group can serve as contract parents for the session with the other half being the children. Experience in reparenting therapy and special training is recommended for those acting as "contract parents."

Tools for Partnerships

It is possible to complete the unmet needs you have left from childhood by becoming more bonded and more separate in your current relationships. Remember, the more completely bonded

you become, the more you will be able to become psychologically separate and able to live interdependently.

• The following checklist can help you find what specific things
  might be missing from your early childhood. You and a partner should go through the list separately and then share with
  each other the items that you have checked. Now review the
  list of reparenting activities given below. Select the ones that
  seem to be what you still need and ask your partner, if it feels
  appropriate, to provide that for you.

REPARENTING CHECKLIST

Bonding That You Missed	*Bonding That You Need*
Being touched or stroked	Getting a massage or back rub taking a warm bath
Being sung to or talked to soothingly	Asking to be held and sung to while listening to soft music
Being given lots of eye contact	Being sung to while having your partner look into your eyes
Being held and rocked	Being rocked
Being given unconditional positive feedback ("I like being with you.")	Being smiled at and given approving non-verbal signals
Being given compliments on how your body looks	Asking for affirmation of your physical appearance

Separation That You Missed	*Separation That You Need*
Exploration support	Joining a support group
Mirroring that recognizes your individuality and specialness	Attending couples' workshops

Separation That You Missed	*Separation That You Need*
Being able to feel connected with people even when you are away from them	Taking separate vacations
Affirmation of your need to set limits and have boundaries	Developing friends of the same sex
Support for taking initiative to do things on your own	Signing up for courses or instruction in a new interest
	Trying initiative tests such as rappeling, ropes courses, etc.
	Planning times to be alone
	Doing a "vision quest" or solo experience in the wilderness
	Learning a new skill that you have always wanted to learn

Case Example

Patty was a member of a therapy group I (Barry) was conducting. One evening she spontaneously reenacted her own birth. At first I didn't know what was happening as she curled up in a fetal position and laid there motionless for a time. Intuitively I covered her with a blanket, and then she started to cry and kick some. I asked the other group members to help me create a womb and a birth canal. Slowly over the next half hour or so, Patty relived her birth process. Here is how she described it:

> I stopped crying to analyze my feelings and suddenly I realized I was in the womb. I could not deny any longer what was happening to me. I said to Barry, 'I'm not born yet!' Now I was more surprised than scared, and support from the group was critical. I knew I did not want to stop. My only awareness was the sound of Barry's voice. He was talking to me about being born, and the sound of his voice was very helpful.

I actually remember not wanting to be born. How could I not want to be born? I was already twenty-six years old. I had my eyes closed and I saw an image of a large hand about to hit me. My fear of being born turned out to be another important step. I realized I really needed to make a decision to be born. It never occurred to me that I had any choice in the matter. Barry told me that I indeed could choose whether or not I wanted to be born. I thought about this for a while and then I asked Barry, 'Are you going to slap me?' When Barry said, 'No,' I experienced a deep sense of relief and made the decision to be born.

Once again I was crying but I still had no tears. My cry was like a yell or a fearful, helpless, uncontrolled scream. I wiggled and pushed until I was completely out of breath and out from under the blanket.

To check out whether or not I had completed my "rebirth" process, Barry asked, 'How do you know you are alive?' My answer to this was beautiful and simple. I said, 'I am breathing and I really feel good.'

Suddenly I felt cold, and Barry wrapped me in a blanket and held me and I felt content and secure. It seemed as if I was being taken care of for the first time in my life. I then experienced all my senses except taste. I was distracted by colors and textures, and I could feel Barry's voice emitting very calm, comforting feelings as he talked to me. Wow! That is the way to communicate with babies. The whole thing was a truly joyful experience!

Following this experience, Patty and I negotiated a parenting contract. For the next several years, I served as her "contract parent," providing her with important bonding experiences and eventually support for becoming autonomous. Patty moved to another city and we formally ended our therapeutic relationship. We are still good friends and correspond or visit when she returns to town. Reparenting contracts need to have beginnings and endings so that people have an awareness of having completed their developmental tasks. This validates their work and acknowledges their growth.

Reparenting contracts can be short- or long-term, depending on the needs and time of the individuals involved. Not all reparenting activities need extensive contracts to be effective. Sometimes in a friendship or relationship, a simple acknowledgment such as "you remind me of my father/sister/mother and I feel close to you because of that" is all that is necessary to acknowledge that unfinished business with other persons is being completed.

CHAPTER EIGHTEEN

New Forms of Relationship

It seems as if everyone is searching for a new form of relationship that is more satisfying and nourishing than what they are used to. We don't even have words to completely describe this relationship. We can try by describing what it is not: it is not co-dependent anymore. But it is more difficult to describe what it is instead.

INTERDEPENDENCY

This new form of relationship that flows out of the process of recovery from co-dependency is an interdependent relationship.

It may look co-dependent, counter-dependent or independent, at times. When you connect with another person at a deep level, you start a new dance together that has many moves in it that flow from one to another. When two people learn to become separate, whole, autonomous people, you no longer need to protect yourselves from each other. You are free to be yourself. You realize that you are loved for who you really are, not for some false image you tried to create. Partners in this kind of relationship dance can weave in and out of deep connection, are not always intimate with each other, and can fight and argue with each other. What makes that possible is commitment and consciousness. For that reason, we prefer to call this form of relationship a *conscious, committed, cooperative relationship.*

The Characteristics of a Conscious, Committed, Cooperative Relationship

In summary form below is a list of the main characteristics of a conscious, committed, cooperative relationship, which include:

- A recognition that behavior patterns based on fears and unhealed wounds from childhood are the enemy, and there is an agreement that the main focus of the relationship is overcoming and healing these core issues.

- A commitment to stay with conflicts until personal awareness and resolution occur.

- A therapeutic function. The word therapy comes from the Greek work *therapea* which means doing the work of the whole. It is a healing *and* a wholing process.

- A discovery process. Your intent is to discover and understand more about yourself and your partner and not to try to change them.

- A basis of self-trust rather than primal trust. Rather than believing that the other won't hurt you, you trust yourself more so that you can be hurt less by your partner and you feel less responsible for hurting your partner. If you say or do anything that unintentionally hurts your partner, you can trust your partner to take care of himself or herself and ask for what s/he wants from you.

- Seeing your partner as your mirror. This helps you see more clearly your deepest parts and the parts of yourself at which you have avoided looking.

- A focus on each person's relationship with himself or herself. The partners agree to cooperate and support the other person's relationship with himself or herself.

- A recognition that children can help you become more self-aware and enable you to deepen your ability to love yourself and others. Children are our greatest teachers.

- Conflicts with children are resolved in ways that don't unduly frustrate a child's search for personal autonomy. You need to give up trying to control your children and instead get to know them and learn from them.

- A recognition that these principles apply to all relationships, including student-teacher, employee-employer, friend-colleague and nation-to-nation relationships. The goal is to help humankind learn to live together in peace and with love.

Nourishing and Toxic Relationships

Not everyone is ready for conscious, committed, cooperative relationships. It is important to assess where you and your partner are in your relationship. There is a spectrum of consciousness and commitment in relationships that extends from nourishing to toxic. The five levels (Bolton 1979) are as follows:

1. *A very nourishing relationship*—high levels of both consciousness and commitment. Each of you contribute greatly to each other's growth.

2. *A mildly nourishing relationship*—lower levels of consciousness or commitment in some areas reduce the contribution you can make to each other's lives.

3. *A noncontributing relationship*—the consciousness and commitment to growth and learning is sufficiently low enough to make little or no contribution to your personal development.

4. *A mildly toxic relationship*—so little consciousness and commitment that each of you feels slightly diminished as a person, and the relationship interferes with your enjoyment of life.

5. *A very toxic relationship*—no noticeable commitment to growth. Instead there are excessive demands, hostility and verbal or physical abuse which is very depleting to both of you.

If you are in relationships that are more toxic or less nourishing than what you are happy with, you will need to determine what you are willing to do to try to move the relationships in a more nourishing direction and determine the willingness of your partner(s) to cooperate with your efforts. If neither of those strategies proves to be successful, then you need to find the courage to end a relationship where you cannot get your needs met.

TOOLS FOR CREATING NEW FORMS OF RELATIONSHIP

Tools for Working Alone

Sometimes it is necessary to take a "time out" in the middle of a conflict in order to think through your reactions and responses. Try this activity to help you get more clarity.

• Think of three things you don't like about your partner that you want him or her to change. Write them on a piece of paper. Then ask yourself, "Where and how am I like that and when do I do the same things?" Write your answers on the paper. Then ask yourself, "Am I willing to change these things in myself?" If the answer is "no," then what right do you have to try to get your partner to change these things?

• If you *do* change these undesirable things in yourself, the other person may be encouraged to change as well. This is the only way to change others—by changing yourself first. Remember that the ultimate state of stuckness is waiting for someone else to change before you can feel better.

Tools for Therapy

Relationship therapy or family therapy is preferable to individual therapy in breaking co-dependency. It is possible to do some individual therapy to become more aware of core issues, but partners have to work together to break their patterns. It is also useful for people in a relationship to have the benefit of a common framework and language that a single therapist can provide.

Couples therapy can also provide an excellent setting to work through the conscious completion of the psychological birth. The therapist can supply the needed support that you didn't get from your parents for each to work through the stuck part of your development. To make this work, the therapist has to build a solid relationship with each partner in order to provide enough bonding and safety for the work to occur. The resolution of the developmental crisis involves everyone feeling okay about themselves and each other. A skilled therapist and willing partners can create the conditions for this completion to occur for either or both of the partners.

It is common for one member in a partnership to "wake up" first and to seek therapy without his/her partner. The task is then to get the missing partner to come to relationship therapy. There is often resistance to this, so here are a few suggestions on how to deal with this resistance.

• Ask your partner to come to therapy to help you. Most partners can't resist this one if they are co-dependent.

• Tell your partner that you are going to talk about him or her and your relationship in therapy, and you want them there to give their view of things. A resistant partner will want to know all that is happening and will be motivated to defend himself or herself.

• Ask your partner to join you for a limited number of sessions (1-3 sessions) to see how therapy might help them. This is a limited enough request that a resistant partner may agree to do it.

• It is not good to issue ultimatums regarding therapy ("or else"). However, a very resistant partner will often need firm limits on what is acceptable to you. If you believe therapy is the only hope for the relationship, then say so and enlist your partner's cooperation. If he or she is unwilling, you know that his or her resistance is more important to them than taking positive steps toward change.

Tools for Support Groups

A group formed with other people in committed relationships can be an important source of support. It is easy to feel very alone and isolated if you are doing this work and most of your friends are not. Meeting occasionally with others who are on a similar path, working toward breaking their co-dependent patterns, can be just what is needed.

If partners have studied this or some other similar framework for understanding co-dependency, it is quite helpful to have them work with each other. The interventions, support and insights of other couples going through the same or a similar process can benefit those doing the helping and those being helped.

It is also useful to split up partners in a group to give the men and women a chance to talk directly with other men and women. Sometimes the support of someone of the same sex is badly needed and hard to find.

Tools for Partnerships

• Knowing a way to learn your important lessons from your intimate relationships can be quite valuable. Jordan and Margaret Paul in their book *Do I Have to Give Up Me to be Loved By You* (1983) suggest key questions partners need to ask each other in each step of the process. Their four-step process is paraphrased below.

> 1. *Exploring what is happening.* The key questions are: Will you describe what you believe has been happening to you, to me, to us? What do you think is going to happen next? What would you like to have happen next? What are you doing that is interfering with the resolution of the conflict? What do you see that I am doing to interfere?
>
> 2. *Exploring your understanding of each other.* Do you feel understood, listened to, respected by me? If not, what do you need from me to feel more of these qualities?
>
> 3. *Exploring your feelings.* How do you feel about our communication so far? What suggestions do you have to improve our communication? How do you feel toward me now? What, if anything, do you need from me in order to feel better about me and what we are doing?
>
> 4. *Exploring Intent.* Are you willing to open up to learning more about me? Do you see me defending a position or open to learning? Do you feel I want to understand you and your feelings? What can I do to improve in this area?

• One of the most important areas in building a cooperative relationship is making and keeping clear agreements. The following is designed to promote these objectives. Take turns reading each rule aloud with your partner. Then put the rule into your own words ("What I think this means is . . ."), give an example of your use or misuse of the rule and ask your partner to comment on the rule. The rules for making and keeping agreements are as follows:

1. Make only agreements you are willing and able to keep. Think carefully about the agreement before making it.

2. Communicate directly any potential broken agreements before they are actually broken (i.e., Call if you know you are going to be late).

3. Speak with good intent. Do not forecast failure for the agreement. Ask, "Is there anything that you can see that might interfere with you keeping this agreement?"

4. If a problem arises, communicate it directly to your partner at the first appropriate opportunity. Never unilaterally break an agreement.

5. Tell the truth responsibly and allow others to do the same (i.e., "The truth for me is . . .").

6. Focus on the problem and the solution. Do not backtrack to find reasons or justifications for the problem.

7. Find the other person *right* for what they are doing instead of trying to show them why they are wrong (i.e.,"I notice you weren't able to do the dishes as you had agreed. Can you tell me what happened?")

8. If someone blames you for breaking an agreement, ask them if they would be willing to forgive you. Also ask them what they want from you to repair the damage.

9. Tell them how you see the problem and give them the solution that you want; then ask them to do the same.

• Another fun and interesting activity involves making a collage of the relationship. Ask each person separately to construct a collage using pictures and headings from old magazines to represent how he or she sees the relationship. Then compare what each created separately and look for points of contact (similarities and differences). A second step would be for a couple to co-create a joint collage to represent how they would like the relationship to be. Collages can be displayed at home as reminders of what each wants or what they want together.

Case Example

Bob and June came to therapy because they had hit a "wall" in their relationship even though they had a conscious, committed relationship. They were unable to work their way through their problem and came to us to gain some additional skills and information.

Bob said, "I don't know what is going on; we are getting on each other's nerves." June said, "I love this man very much but lately he has been doing things that really push my buttons. I am starting to withdraw from him because of this and I want to find out why."

It seemed that each person was facing new challenges in his or her life and this was causing them to be more tense. Also, they had gotten close enough in their relationship to let down some of their barriers and be more vulnerable with each other. The added tension each was feeling was causing them to be more critical of each other. They were starting to say and do things to each other that were touching previously protected narcissistic wounds.

June was staying at home caring for two small children (ages one and five) and feeling overwhelmed by the demands of the children. She was also feeling overwhelmed by her internal reactions related to her own childhood that parenting was bringing up. Bob was less available for June than usual because he was trying to get his business established. They were missing the support they once felt from each other and did not seem to know how to get it under the present conditions.

We worked with them at several levels. First, we helped them find ways to structure more time together and ways to get them to cooperate and support each other more. However, we knew that there were other forces and issues to be dealt with. We explored with them the so-called "edges" in their relationship. These are the things they believed they couldn't say or do in their relationship.

Through this approach, we were able to find several areas in their relationship where they were co-dependent and counterdependent. These included some important things they needed to say to each other about their sexual needs. Bob was afraid to ask for sex with June for fear that she would perceive this as pressure or a demand and then withdraw or reject him. Also, there were secrets they had kept from each other about their masturbation habits and sexual fantasies. Being able to talk openly about all this was frightening to them but also brought them closer together. It also brought up another level of woundings from their early childhood for both of them. With our guidance, they were able to help each other heal some of these wounds by listening to each other, by trying to understand, and by holding and nurturing each other when the old feelings started to surface.

After about six sessions, Bob called to cancel their next session by saying that they were having so much fun together and wanted to take a vacation from therapy for a while. We wholeheartedly supported this idea and said we would welcome them back for a "tune-up" if they needed one.

Bob and June were both eager to have an interdependent relationship and had a clear vision of what it would be like for them. This vision helped them to create what they wanted and also supported their exploration of what worked and didn't work. These kinds of collaborative, cooperative efforts between partners in a relationship are important in working through the bonding/separation issues so that a deeper, more fluid relationship can be developed.

CHAPTER NINETEEN

Healing The Co-dependent Society

HEALING SOCIETY BY HEALING YOURSELF

The idea of trying to change a whole society, especially one that is a dominator society, is awesome. Where do you begin? The most difficult place to start, it seems, would be in institutions. There are so many people involved, and bureaucracies steadfastly resist change unless they are at the edge of collapse. Actually, the place to start is with yourself.

Once you realize that you are co-dependent and admit that it is making your life difficult, if not miserable, you have done the most important thing. From there the path to recovery is clearer (although not always easier) because now you have a vision of something better. A 12-step program or a support group is almost essential at this stage. Either can provide you with allies who have similar visions and can provide reinforcement for your vision if it wavers. The suggestions related to therapy and how to work on this alone found in this book will also support you and allow you to be in charge of your own healing. This is an important issue. Remember, it is easy to create co-dependent relationships with support groups and therapists. Taking personal charge of your journey to inter-dependence is imperative.

Healing Society Through Committed Relationships

Chapter Eighteen discussed new forms of relationships and how they can be used to heal old wounds and complete de-velopmental issues so that growth can become a primary re-lationship focus. Committed relationships are different from co-dependent relationships because the commitment is not just to the other person but also to oneself. The personal and spir-itual growth of each individual is of primary importance. In-terdependent relationships also have a different focus in that the commitment is not to the *form* but to the *process*. Commit-ments stress contracts and agreements that support safety, se-curity and predictability while the partners are working together on healing themselves and each other. The emphasis on partnership supports the move toward co-creation and ser-vice in committed couples. The strength and clarity of two united people creates a synergy that can be channeled into projects of great size. This is not unlike the last step in the 12-step program for addictions, which calls for people to carry the message to others and practice the principles in all their affairs.

Many clinics, institutes, businesses and organizations are being formed by committed partners who find that they want to extend the dimensions of their relationship out into the com-munity or world.

Healing Society Through Community

Even committed relationships are limited in some ways. Indi-viduals are able to help each other in partnership to the extent that they can provide mirroring, nurturing, support and healing for each other. The degree to which they are able to be present physically and emotionally also limits how much they can help each other. Your partner may travel, get sick or have a conflicting schedule, so it isn't always practical to expect his or her constant physical presence. Also, committed relationships have to do with the multifaceted, multidimensional nature of humans. People have so *many* different parts or sides to them that it is unrealistic to expect one other person to share exactly the same parts and sides and to mirror them back. We need committed relationships with many different people to mirror us, to provide feedback and to partner with us in ways a beloved intimate can't. A support community of friends helps to serve this function. Finally, your partner may also have his or her own issues surfacing, thus making it difficult for him or her to help you with your issues, at times. Again, you may need a support group or network of friends to help you, at times.

Community has become a popular term that replaces what used to be called "extended family"—the aunts, uncles, cousins, grandparents and other relatives who lived in close proximity and made up the social circle. Community provides the same kind of social and emotional support, except that you have more choice about the membership. A good definition for community comes from M. Scott Peck (1987) in his book *The Different Drum: Community Making and Peace*. Community, as he describes it, is a group of people committed to inclusivity, to group process, to governance by consensus, to authenticity and realness, to self-reflection, to safety for group members and to support for resolving conflicts with wisdom and grace. Peck sees community making as a four-stage developmental process:

1. *Pseudocommunity*, the first stage, is artificial. The relationships are shallow, and interactions are based on conformity and the pretense that everyone thinks and behaves alike. Conflict, true feelings and acknowledgment of individual differences are distinctly avoided. This period of pretense, very similar to co-dependency, exists until group members reach their limit on pretense. Then conflict erupts and the group moves into chaos.

2. *Chaos* is characterized by fighting, struggle and open evidence of individual differences. It parallels the stage of counter-dependency. In this stage, the recognized "leader" of pseudocommunity may be deposed by "secondary leaders" who try to organize the chaos back into pseudocommunity. The only way out of chaos is what Peck calls emptiness.

3. *Emptiness* is the most critical stage of community. Here members are required to remove their barriers to communication and to speak honestly. Feelings of pain, sorrow or sadness may flow freely at this point, as people openly acknowledge their brokenness. Prejudices, expectations, preconceptions, the need to control, ideologies, and the need to heal, convert or fix are all put aside. The key in this stage, which parallels the stage of independence, is that the group be able to embrace not only the positive aspects of life but also the negative aspects. When the group allows the artificiality of the pseudocommunity to die, then the group moves into true community.

4. *True community*, the last stage, is the place where interdependence can operate and where members can be their True Selves. True community, especially as modeled in 12-step programs, supports individuals who want to change their lives.

Healing Society Through Servant Leadership

The shift from co-dependency to interdependency in business and industry is beginning to appear in different forms of organizational change based on the concept of "servant leadership." This concept comes directly from Christ and his Holy Thursday act of washing the feet of his disciples. This pre-Good Friday event, mentioned previously in Chapter Three, created the foundation for servant leadership as an emerging organizational movement. The basic idea in servant leadership is one of mutual participation—participation in decisions, risk-taking, management of resources, reward, problems and successes. Leadership is a role that can be filled by anyone with the skills appropriate for the task, and it changes as needs and circumstances change. It allows for the more effective utilization of people and their skills. The servant leadership movement is now emerging in a number of different places.

Robert Greenleaf (1977) is one of the more noted scholars who has been developing this concept. He draws support for servant leadership from a broad spectrum of thoughts that include Eastern philosophies, psychology, business, organizations, churches, education and foundations. His analysis of systems is quite similar to Eisler's partnership/dominator model. He refers to the dominator model as "hierarchical" and the partnership model as "primus."

Other roots of the servant leadership movement are less visible than Robert Greenleaf. They often are found in middle or upper management positions where individuals bring change to work from their own personal paths, such as a 12-step program, meditation, running and fitness, personal growth seminars or other activities designed to transform people. These innovative people often integrate their new personal perspectives into their work, extending support for their growth to the work environment.

TOOLS FOR HEALING THE CO-DEPENDENT SOCIETY

Tools for Working Alone

• Review the following inventory to determine how open your office, business or place of work might be to change. Based on the results, decide what changes you want to make in your work space.

THE OPENNESS TO CHANGE INVENTORY

Directions: Place a check in the column that best represents your perception.

Perception	Never	Sometimes	Usually	Always
1. I have direct input into the rules that are made in this organization.				
2. There are many rules in this organization that restrict my freedom.				
3. Important decisions are made by top administration.				
4. I am consulted on decisions that affect me directly.				
5. I have direct access to information and decisions passed down from the top.				
6. When I want an answer to something, there are many people with whom I have to check.				
7. The goals and purposes of this organization are determined through input from all those involved in the organization.				
8. I do not have direct input into goals and purposes of the organization.				
9. Information and important decisions are shared in face-to-face meetings where everyone is free to express their opinions and feelings.				

Perception	Never	Sometimes	Usually	Always
10. Important information and decisions are communicated in memos, policy letters, telephone calls or other indirect means.				
11. I have the power to make the decisions that affect me most directly.				
12. When I have a conflict with a supervisor or administrator, I feel that I lose.				
13. The approved procedures and schedules are rigidly followed in this organization.				
14. I am free to change what I am doing in response to the needs of my customers/clients.				
15. Managers, supervisors and staff seem to be working together toward common goals and objectives.				
16. My job description tells me exactly what I can and can't do as an employee.				
17. I am encouraged to "wear as many hats" as the situation calls for.				

The scoring system is set up to insure that you do not unconsciously answer the questions in such a way so as to achieve a "desired" score. The "value" of each of the 17 items is tabulated according to the tables below:

For item numbers 1, 4, 5, 7, 9, 11, 14, 15, and 17, score them as follows:

Never = 1   Sometimes = 2   Usually = 3   Always = 4

Total Score A _____

For item numbers 2, 3, 6, 8, 10, 12, 13, and 16, score them as follows:

Never = 4   Sometimes = 3   Usually = 2   Always = 1

Total Score B _____

Grand Total Score (A + B) _____

Your organization's Openness to Change Score can be determined by reading the interpretation below. If your Grand Total Score was:

17-26 There is not much change possible at this time in your organization.
27-36 Proceed slowly with caution.
37-46 Plan carefully for small changes.
47-56 Build a support base first, and be aware of doubletalk.
57-66 Openness to change is apparent.
67 + The sky's the limit.

• Review the following list of qualities that many employers believe are essential in hiring employees. See if you can identify which of these characteristics have co-dependent potential:

   1) High-level organizational ability

   2) Competence at a wide variety of tasks and the ability to learn additional ones quickly

   3) Stability and resistance to panic

4) Skill at diplomacy and emotional manipulation

5) Resilience with a high tolerance to pain

6) High energy, with good resistance to fatigue

7) Good administrative skills

8) The ability to defer gratification indefinitely

9) Crisis intervention skills

10) Strong sense of morality (A sense of right and wrong is crucial in this person's thinking.)

11) Loyalty and a willingness to put the needs of an important group before his or her own (It therefore helps if she is out of touch with her own needs and feelings.)

12) Capacity to never ask "What's in this for me?"

13) The ability to do enormous amounts of work for a minimal payoff

14) High level of nursing and care-taking skills

15) Tendency toward overachievement leading to the ability to work consistently at 120% of capacity

16) Gives low priority to sexual needs and feelings

17) Has physical symptoms as a result of repression

18) Low self-esteem with dependent personality

Tools for Therapy

• Join a therapy group. Ask your therapist if he or she is willing to assume the role of facilitator rather than therapist and facilitate a community-making process as part of your group's structure. Your therapist must be willing to relinquish control during the process if it is to work. Otherwise, pseudocommunity might remain intact.

Tools for Support Groups

• Join a 12-step program and observe the components of its structure. Transfer this experience to other parts of your life such as your family, primary relationship and workplace.

- Ask members of your support group to create a community-making process using the guidelines given in Peck's book on community making.

Tools for Partnerships

- Examine your relationship for evidence of counter-dependent behavior with regard to community. For instance, do you reach out to others to get your needs met and to avoid getting them met in your committed relationships? Identify groups (formal and informal) to which you belong. List what needs each group fulfills. Determine whether or not your partner could fill some of those needs. Many people who are afraid of the intimacy of a committed relationship will evade intimacy and its challenge by joining groups practicing pseudocommunity. Here they try to get some of their unmet needs fulfilled without risking intimacy, which means they are avoiding dealing with many of their real issues.

- Examine your primary relationship for evidence of co-dependent behavior with regard to community. For instance, do you reach out just to your partner to get your needs met and avoid getting any met through community? Identify personal needs that continually are not met in your primary relationship. Determine where in community you might get those needs fulfilled. Discuss these needs with your partner and make a plan for fulfilling each of your unmet personal needs in a community setting.

Case Example

Dave's low point in life came one rainy evening in the park near where he used to live before his divorce. He had lost his job, his wife and children, his savings, and was down to his guitar and a quart of whiskey. He arrived at the park already drunk and planned to spend the evening sipping his bottle and strumming his guitar. As he moved to a sheltered spot to sit, he stumbled in a hole. Over he went. The bottle slipped out of his hand while his guitar flew off to one side and bounced off a large rock nearby. He found himself face down in the mud, his bottle shattered, guitar broken and himself at the end of his rope. He sobbed quietly and beat his fists weakly on the ground saying, "Great Spirit, please help me." Dave, a Native American, had no other place to turn. He decided to return to the teachings of his culture and began to seek a spiritual dimension in his life. He went home, cleaned himself up and began to ask for guidance from the Great Spirit.

He eventually joined AA and broke his addiction to alcohol. He also returned to his Native American roots and sought the wisdom of their ancient teachings. In these two groups, he found surprisingly similar principles based on the partnership model. Through them he found the strength to restore himself to dignity and created a new life, found a new wife and family and a new job.

He felt great peace in his personal life and yearned to bring it into his professional life. He made exploratory inquiries about introducing his personal perspective and experience into his management group, but his supervisors were skeptical. Finally, one day he just decided to do it. He felt sure the principles would work and decided he would rather ask for forgiveness, if necessary, than ask for permission first.

He found the principles to be as effective as he had anticipated. He first implemented them in his own group. Then other company groups heard about his approach and they tried it. Eventually six of the seven company groups in his plant of almost 4,000 employees adopted his partnership/community model of management. Dave recently trained national and international managers from other plants in his company, extending his personal experience out into the world.

CHAPTER TWENTY

How We Changed Our Co-dependent Patterns

This chapter is divided into our individual stories before we met and after we met.

JANAE'S STORY

I was the first daughter, second of five children born to a farm couple. My mother tried to nurse me but couldn't. I lost weight steadily until the doctor recommended bottle feeding. At that point, she got pregnant again and gave birth to my sister when I was eleven months old. During my mother's hospitalization, my grandmother kept me. I remember my mother telling me numerous times how I refused to have anything to do with her for over a week after she and my sister came home from the hospital. I was so hurt and angry that I would not even look at her. Two years later a second sister came. By this time, my mother had four children under the age of seven and needed help from neighborhood girls to take care of us all. I remember my childhood being lonely. My mother was always busy and we didn't visit much with our extended family. My main source of joy and friendship was visiting the many animals and their babies that we had on the farm.

During my early childhood, my father struggled to support us by farming. He worked long hours during much of the year. My parents grew most of our food. My mother pasteurized milk, made butter, canned, froze, and sewed all of the clothes for herself, my sisters and me. Somehow she had time to do laundry, cleaning and care for children. We had a series of "mother's helpers" during the summers to watch us while she did her farm-wife work.

I don't remember having much of a feeling of connection with my mother. I don't think I ever forgave her for abandoning me at my sister's birth, and I never really bonded to her again. As more and more children kept coming, I gave up hope of getting my bonding needs met. I remember feeling closer to my father. He was more available than my mother after my first sister's birth, so I felt more bonded to him. His availability during that period helped me separate from my mother but left me stuck in counter-dependency. I got approval for self-sufficiency and caretaking behaviors, and quickly took on parenting and adult responsibilities. I became the achiever or "hero" in the famiy.

When I was twelve, my mother killed herself and my five-year-old brother. We found them in the car with the garage full of carbon monoxide fumes. I was devastated by the loss of my little brother as he was the one person in the family to whom I felt close. My maternal relatives abandoned us in shame after her suicide, making our lives even more isolated. After my mother's death, I took over the role of "farm wife," doing many of her jobs in addition to my school work. By high school graduation I had pretty well mastered the role. During my junior year in high school, however, my co-dependent needs began to surface. I had a boyfriend and planned to get married right after I graduated from college. I majored in home economics and graduated in three years with honors.

During a summer at a human development institute in another state in my senior year in college, a whole new world opened to me. Here I had my first glimpse of another way of life, with values opposite to those of my midwestern farm life. I was exposed to people and ideas that supported openness, exploration, curiosity and conscious parenting. I returned to college, to my family and my boyfriend with a vision of something new and better. Nowhere, however, was there any support for this new vision. The whole system (steeped in the dominator model) encouraged and rewarded passivity, conformity and co-dependency. My boyfriend and I eventually broke up. After graduation, I found a job teaching in a small farm town much like the one where I grew up, where the rural patterns of roles and relationships felt familiar. Immediately I began dating Herb, the agriculture teacher in the school, and four months later I married him.

By this time, the strain of maintaining a counter-dependent facade had taken its toll. I quickly surrendered to my co-dependent needs for symbiosis and protection. I turned over my savings to Herb, along with the management of it. I got pregnant quickly and quit my teaching job at the end of my first year.

In my marriage, I assumed the very passive role I had seen my mother take in her relationship with my father. I projected my masculine part onto Herb, as we created a very traditional relationship with rigid roles. I cooked, sewed, cleaned and worked at being the perfect wife, while he managed the money, enforced the discipline and made the rules. We had two sons, five years apart. We lived away from both our families much of the time, so I had only my sons and Herb for support. I was very lonely but was discouraged by Herb from venturing outside our nuclear family for anything.

With all my background in child care and family life, I gave the wife/mother role everything I had. I was determined to create a family with the closeness I had always wanted. My needs for closeness and protection were so intense that I worked even harder when there were rough spots in the relationship.

After nineteen years of struggle to get my emotional needs met in these unhealthy ways, I found myself physically exhausted and psychologically empty. I felt as though I was dying and that I had totally lost myself. In a state of crisis, I sought counseling. The therapy helped me validate my needs and gave me support for making changes in myself and in my relationship. I joined a therapy group which helped me see how universal my circumstances were and supported me in making changes in my life. This also revived my vision from my college days of something better for myself. I also read dozens of books and enrolled in personal growth seminars and workshops. I found a support system at Overeaters Anonymous (my family's addiction) and in university classes when I decided to begin graduate school. All these experiences helped support my vision of a better kind of life.

Herb and I went for counseling together a few times. I hoped that we would be able to transform our relationship into something larger and richer. After two or three sessions, however, it became obvious that my dream would not happen. Herb really wanted me to return to the old form of relationship. We divorced eventually and I moved on with my life.

My advisor at the university had suggested that I begin doctoral work, but I decided to do a year of graduate work first. During that year I attended a seminar with Jean Houston and then enrolled in her Mystery School training program in New York, where I met Barry.

BARRY'S STORY

I was the first-born male in an upwardly mobile working class family with a large extended family in a small town. According to my mother, I had an easy birth (30-minute labor) with somewhat tenuous bonding. I was a "failure-to-thrive" infant and almost died at six weeks due to a lack of nourishment. Further bonding was provided by my paternal grandmother at that time and later, at ten months, by a very nurturing nanny.

My father was either absent, injured or sick during my early childhood. He worked long hours, was hurt in a work-related accident and had chronic respiratory illnesses. He was not there to support me in developing independence from those to whom I was bonded. I found myself enmeshed in a co-dependent extended family.

My later childhood was dominated by "be careful" messages and attempts to please my "mothers." I remember in grades 1-4, my grandmother gave me a dime for each "A" in deportment I received, reinforcing conforming behavior. I also remember my mother yelling at me occasionally and my father rescuing me later by telling me privately that my mother didn't mean what she said. My grandfather rescued my father from his parenting responsibilities by spending time with me when my father was unavailable.

Adolescence was rocky, but by high school I began to gain some self-confidence. As a sophomore I was picked for the junior varsity basketball team and ended high school lettering in basketball and baseball. I also joined De Molay and worked my way up to the highest office in two years.

Fran and I met on a blind date while I was a sophomore in college. She was just finishing high school. After two and a half years of dating, we got married and began recreating the co-dependent patterns with which we were both familiar. We both had trouble with intimacy and managed to avoid each other by arranging conflicting work and school schedules for the first six years of marriage.

During my graduate training and the period immediately following graduation, our marriage started falling apart. We had two small children by now, which fulfilled one of Fran's major dreams. I found that I wanted more intimacy than she was comfortable with but she seemed willing to learn. That phase of our relationship carried us through another eight to ten years. I think neither of us could face the prospect of being alone, so the fear of loneliness kept us together. During that time we tried to build a more cooperative relationship. I learned to cook and take care of myself around the home and she learned to be out in the world. I also went through outpatient reparenting therapy for about three years and filled in some of the major gaps in my development. I developed more basic trust, stopped seeing myself as "special" (and therefore different from others) and developed more object constancy. As we made these changes, we came to see some of the areas of incompatability we had failed to notice: our goals were far different, our world view was different and we didn't find that our contact together nourished us very much any more. We decided to divorce and find our ways separately.

After living alone for several months and dating several women, I started dating my old friend, Barbara, who had been divorced for about a year. We found we had much in common. Eight months later we eloped to Reno. I felt like I had met my soul mate. Barbara was my projected idealized feminine part and I was her projected idealized masculine part. Our relationship involved each of us trying to live up to the projections of the other one. Problems occurred when either one failed to live up to one of these projections. I found myself becoming more and more wooden and one-dimensional as the problems increased.

Barbara discovered she was an adult survivor of incest and suffered from bulimia, an eating disorder. She worked very hard to deal with these problems and I worked very hard doing what I was trained to do: take care of her. I became a butler in our relationship, always trying to please and not get upset. I went into more therapy to work my way out of this role and began asserting my independence in our relationship. I also realized that I was still resisting Barbara's problems and was trying to control her and manipulate her back into the idealized image I had of her.

Finally, I found the key: surrender. Surrender had a masculine and a feminine form for me to learn. The masculine form involved my willingness to take charge of myself without guilt, and the feminine form involved my willingness to receive or accept Barbara and her problems without resistance. Therapy helped me with the masculine form and I learned the feminine form with Barbara. Together these two concepts helped me break some of my major co-dependent patterns.

Unfortunately, I didn't have much time to enjoy these gains

in my relationship with Barbara because about six weeks after my breakthrough experience with her, she was killed in a skiing accident. My life was shattered. I was alone and I wasn't sure I wanted to live. This was the real test of my learning. I had to take charge of my life and I had to reclaim the feminine part I had projected on Barbara.

I set out to find new allies to help me complete my sacred marriage (marriage of the inner masculine and feminine). Jean Houston taught me how to find my beloved within and Robert Bly taught me how to find my deep masculine "wild man." Also I enrolled in Jean Houston's year-long Mystery School to get additional support for my integration. I found more than I expected at the Mystery School because that is where I met Janae.

OUR STORY

How We Met

JANAE

The Mystery School training was a period of great growth for me. Leaving my "housewife" existence, I dared to drive 300 miles into Chicago and fly from there to New York. I had flown just once before in my life, so this was a big leap for me. At the training I met people from all parts of the country who were in many different professions. The broad range of studies about the spiritual teachings of ancient cultures, combined with the diverse background of the participants and the spirit of adventure, literally exploded my horizons. So many possibilities opened to me that I began to feel confused about the next stage of my life.

After my divorce, my sons had both decided to attend school in another state, so I was free, at the age of forty-one, to begin a new life. I felt drawn to the Native American teachings and finally decided that I would do a vision quest. I was at this point, considering how and where I would do that when Barry and I bumped into each other while dancing at Mystery School.

During a chat later about the incident, he asked me if I was coming to Colorado soon. If I did (which was a pretty remote possibility at that time), he invited me to visit him.

A subsequent letter encouraging me to visit him in Colorado came on the same day as I received two other messages about going to Colorado. This was a clear signal that I should go. A big snow in Colorado, however, prevented me from doing the planned vision quest. I did attend a weekend class that Barry was teaching, thinking I would be a spectator. Instead, he invited me to *teach* with him! It was like a dream come true, as I had yearned for a partner who shared my interests. The ten days we spent together were some of the most incredible of my life as we discovered area after area of mutual interest and many common dreams. After so many years in a relationship that wasn't what I wanted and having so clear a vision of what I did want, it was easy to say "yes" to life. I made arrangements to move myself to Colorado as soon as possible.

BARRY

Although we had been going to Mystery School weekends once a month since February, we did not actually connect until September. On Friday evening, everyone engaged in free-form dancing before the evening program began and as I spun around, my arm hit someone in the chest. I apologized and moved on. The next morning I saw Janae and again apologized briefly. We hardly spoke another word to each other all weekend, but somehow I felt her presence when we were near each other during the weekend.

When we were preparing to leave on Sunday afternoon, I gave Janae a hug and told her I was attracted to her and wanted to get to know her better. I said, "There doesn't seem to be much time to get to know people during these weekends. Is there any chance you might be coming to Colorado any time soon?" Her response was guarded.

On the plane back to Colorado I reflected on my boldness and decided to write her a letter explaining that since Barbara's death I was taking uncharacteristic risks by sharing my thoughts and feelings more openly. I received a letter back in a week, thanking me for my honesty and vulnerability and announcing that she would be coming to Colorado in the next month to do a vision quest.

She had planned to spend ten days visiting in Colorado. After four days together, however, we knew we were going to be married. The match of our physical, emotional, intellectual and spiritual bodies was unbelievable and at the same time undeniable. We made plans for her to move out to Colorado and planned a Thanksgiving wedding. This was the beginning of an incredible journey together.

The Journey to Interdependence

JANAE

Although I had been separated from Herb for a year, my divorce was final only four months prior to my marriage to Barry. I had planned to develop my independence more after the divorce. Meeting Barry changed that. I decided I would have to learn that while in a relationship.

For me, the early days of our marriage were about bonding. The warmth, openness and deep capacities for feeling that I found in Barry allowed me to reveal the deep wounds from my relationship with Herb. Gradually I found unhealed losses surfacing from my childhood. With the aid of my therapist, and with support from Barry, I was able to finally acknowledge my lack of bonding. Barry held me, stroked me and provided many hours of nurturing during our first months together. I was able to consciously project "nurturing parent" on him in order to heal my bonding wounds.

We worked at creating a partnership, sharing responsibilities—cooking, driving and decision making. Within a few months, I began to work for my doctorate degree so that I could function as a full partner. This required that I leap into a whole new world and required that I break many old patterns and the rigid roles I had learned. Barry's mentoring supported my buried dreams of achievement, as well as my need to be a separate person. Our intense bonding work, combined with his support for autonomy, really helped me complete a lot of the unfinished business from my early childhood.

BARRY

When we got together, I still had lots of grieving to do over Barbara's death. What really helped was that Janae was willing to listen to me talk openly about my loss, and many an evening she held me as I cried. She also did not rush me through this and encouraged me to take as long as I needed to heal those wounds. Barbara's death triggered many other unhealed loss issues from my childhood, so the healing also involved dealing with many co-dependent patterns.

As we did the healing and bonding, I found it easier to ask for what I wanted from Janae and I became very aware of my projections on her. I also found that the letting go and surrendering that I had learned to do with Barbara had remained with me. When I started resisting something Janae said or did, I would remember and surrender to her.

We have had our share of fights, but we get through them now very quickly, usually in an hour or less. One of the keys to making our relationship work has been our commitment to making the resolution of all conflicts our first priority. That is something we don't put aside, even if it comes at an inconvenient time. Our first commitment is to helping each other heal our wounds and completing the unfinished business we each brought into the relationship. Fortunately, we both agreed that this was the only way we could get all that we wanted from our relationship.

We also agreed that we both wanted a partnership lifestyle that enabled us to integrate our work and our relationship. We frequently spend 24 hours a day with each other for as long as a week or two, and then we take time to be by ourselves or with others. But we never seem to lose the deep love connection we have with each other. We are free to be co-dependent, counter-dependent, independent or interdependent with each other. When sometimes we want different things, we are secure enough as individuals to resolve our conflicts and get what we want.

A New Understanding of Co-dependency

BARRY

In the context of our integrated relationship, we decided to start an institute to work together toward world peace. We found the context of conflict resolution and creative leadership broad enough to include all of our interests. After a year of preparation, The Colorado Institute for Conflict Resolution and Creative Leadership (CICRCL) was officially opened. We started with an eight-day international conference for three hundred people. We had a group of about 20-30 volunteers and very little money, working to develop new approaches to conflict resolution. We lost money on our first conference and gradually started putting more and more of our own money and time into the Institute to help create paying jobs for others who shared our vision but had no money to contribute.

We woke up one day and realized that, without knowing it, we had created a co-dependent organization. Even though we used group decision making in the Institute from the beginning, the unequal contribution of money created a hierarchy. We noticed that we were making more of the decisions and others were deferring to us as the leaders. We saw that even though we had cleared our major co-dependent patterns from our relationship, we were not conscious enough to see the same patterns in the organization we had helped to create. It was a very humbling experience indeed. Undoubtedly, we have many more lessons to be learned in this area.

Rather than continue to create a dysfunctional organization, we did the only thing we were capable of doing: we stopped what we were doing. The reactions of those who had developed co-dependent relationships with us and the Institute were predictable. Some people were very angry at us and spent considerable energy making us wrong. When we refused to engage their energy, much of it dissipated, and some people then began to look at their own unfinished business and their co-dependent patterns. A few seemed to flee into counter-dependency as angry victims.

JANAE

For me, CICRCL became a child of our union—birthed out of our common vision, nursed during its first fragile months and supported faithfully with all of our resources. Of course, I reacted with all of my old parenting responses. I focused on taking care of the needs of other people: creating paying jobs for others while working without pay myself, putting on workshops and organizing conferences and doing promotional work. All this was for the "good of CICRCL."

It wasn't until I was near exhaustion from my own unmet needs that I realized I had taken on the role of co-dependent "mother." I was astounded at the ease with which I had done this and at the similarity of my behavior in the parenting of my children. I was also astounded at my inability to see the presence of the patterns. Once the patterns penetrated my awareness and I could see the dysfunctionality, it was easy to let go and hope that we could discover a new form of partnership at an organizational level.

Our Perspective On Relationships

As you know now from our story, we both came from ordinary circumstances and from typical kinds of families in which the parents did the best they could. We want to acknowledge our experiences in these families as great learnings for ourselves and, now, as a source for helping others understand themselves. These experiences have helped us recognize our woundings and our struggle to create something better as links to our universal humanness, as part of our connection to the experiences of others.

We acknowledge that this path requires faith, courage and a higher vision of what is possible. Once the commitment to this higher vision is firm, breaking free of co-dependency is not just an option. It is inevitable, if we are to become whole.

Bibliography

Arguelles, Jose. 1987. *The Mayan Factor*. Santa Fe: Bear & Co.

Beattie, Melody. 1987. *Co-dependent No More*. New York: Harper & Row.

Black, Claudia. 1981. *It Will Never Happen to Me*. Denver, CO: M.A.C. Printing and Publication Division.

Bolton, Robert. 1979. *People Skills*. New York: Simon and Schuster.

Bradshaw, John. 1988. *Bradshaw On: The Family*. Deerfield Beach, FL: Health Communications, Inc.

Bradshaw, John. 1989. *Healing the Shame that Binds You*. Pompano Beach, FL: Health Communications, Inc.

Clemes, H. & Bean, R. 1981. *Self-Esteem: The Key to Your Child's Well-Being*. New York: G. P. Putnam & Sons.

Coopersmith, S. 1967. *The Antecedents of Self-Esteem*. San Francisco: W. H. Freeman & Co.

Eisler, Riane. 1987. *The Chalice & The Blade*. San Francisco: Harper & Row.

Fenell, David & Weinhold, Barry. 1989. *Counseling Families: An Introduction to Marriage and Family Therapy*. Denver, CO: Love Publishing Co.

Fingarette, Herbert. 1988. *Heavy Drinking: The Myth of Alcoholism as a Disease*. Berkeley, CA: University of California Press.

Greenleaf, Robert. 1977. *Servant Leadership*. New York: Pauliot Press.

Griffin, Susan. 1978. *Woman and Nature*. New York: Harper & Row.

Halpern, Howard. 1982. *How To Break Your Addiction To A Person*. New York: McGraw-Hill Book Company.

Hay, Louise. 1984. *You Can Heal Your Life*. Farmingdale, NY: Coleman Publishing.

Hendricks, Gay & Weinhold, Barry. 1982. *Transpersonal Approaches to Counseling and Psychotherapy.* Denver, CO: Love Publishing Co.

Houston, Jean. 1982. *The Possible Human.* Los Angeles: J. P. Tarcher.

Jacobs, Caryl. 1984. "Patterns of Violence: A Feminist Perspective on the Regulation of Pornography," *Harvard Women's Law Journal.* 7:5-55.

Jones, Alexander. 1966. *The Jerusalem Bible.* Garden City, NY: Doubleday, Inc.

Kaplan, Louise J. 1978. *Oneness and Separateness: From Infant to Individual.* New York: Simon and Schuster.

Karpman, Steven. 1968. "Fairytales and Script Drama Analysis," *Transitional Analysis Bulletin.* 7:39-43.

Klaus, Marshall & Kennell, John. 1976. *Maternal Infant Bonding.* St. Louis: The C. V. Mosby Company.

Kübler-Ross, Elizabeth. 1969. *On Death and Dying.* New York: Macmillan.

Larsen, Earnie. 1985. *Stage II Recover: Life Beyond Addiction.* San Francisco: Harper & Row.

Magid, K. & McKelvey, C. 1988. *High Risk.* New York: Bantam Books.

Mahler, Margaret. 1968. *On Human Symbiosis and the Vicissitudes of Individuation.* New York: International University Press.

Miller, Alice. 1983. *For Your Own Good.* New York: Farrar, Straus, Giroux.

Mindell, Arnold. 1987. *The Dreambody in Relationships.* Boston: Sigo Press.

Pagels, Elaine. 1979. *The Gnostic Gospels.* New York: Random House.

Paul, Jordan & Paul, Margaret. 1983. *Do I Have To Give Up Me To Be Loved By You?* Minneapolis: CompCare Publications.

Pearce, Joseph C. 1977. *Magical Child.* New York: E. P. Dutton.

Pearce, Joseph C. 1985. *Magical Child Matures.* New York: E. P. Dutton.

Peck, M. Scott. 1978. *The Road Less Travelled.* New York: Simon and Schuster.

Peck, M. Scott. 1987. *The Different Drum: Community Making and Peace.* New York: Simon and Schuster.

Peele, Stanton. 1989. *The Diseasing of America: How the Addiction Industry Captured Our Soul.* Lexington, MA: Lexington Books.

Roszak, Theodore. 1979. *Person-Planet.* Garden City, NY: Anchor Press.

Russell, Peter. 1983. *The Global Brain.* Los Angeles: J. P. Tarcher.

Satir, Virginia. 1972. *Peoplemaking.* Palo Alto, CA: Science & Behavior Books.

Schaef, Anne Wilson. 1981. *Women's Reality.* Minneapolis: Winston Press.

Schaef, Anne Wilson. 1986. *Co-Dependence Misunderstood—Mistreated.* New York: Harper & Row.

Schaef, Anne Wilson. 1987. *When Society Becomes An Addict*. San Francisco: Harper & Row.

Schiff, Jacqui, et al. 1975. *The Cathexis Reader*. New York: Harper & Row.

Sheehy, Gail. 1981. *Pathfinders*. New York: Bantam Books.

Starhawk. 1979. "Witchcraft & Women's Culture," in *Womanspirit Rising*, C. Christ & J. Plaskow, Eds. New York: Harper & Row.

Steiner, Claude. 1974. *Scripts People Live*. New York: Grove Press.

Subby, Robert. 1984. "Inside the Chemically Dependent Marriage: Denial Manipulation," in *Co-Dependency: An Emerging Issue*. Pompano Beach, FL: Health Communications.

Subby, Robert & Friel, John. 1984. "Co-dependency: A Paradoxical Dependency," in *Co-Dependency: An Emerging Issue*. Pompano Beach, FL: Health Communications.

von Franz, Marie-Louis and Hillman, James. 1979. *Lectures on Jung's Typology*. Irving, TX: Spring Publications, Inc.

Weinhold, Barry & Hillferty, Judy. 1983. "The Self-Esteem Matrix: A Tool for Elementary Counselors," *Elementary School Guidance and Counseling*. 17:243-251.

Weinhold, Barry. 1988. *Playing Grown-Up Is Serious Business: Breaking Free of Addictive Family Patterns*. Walpole, NH: Stillpoint International.

Whitfield, Charles. 1987. *Healing The Child Within*. Deerfield Beach, FL: Health Communications, Inc.

Zaleski, Philip. 1984. "A New Age Interview: Elizabeth Kübler-Ross," *New Age Journal*. November, pp 39-44.

Notice

You may contact Barry and Janae Weinhold for information on:

- Training workshops and presentations in your area
- Programs offered through their Family Training Center
- Programs offered through the Colorado Institute for Conflict Resolution and Creative Leadership

Send your inquiries to:

C I C R C L
330 West Unitah
Suite 171
Colorado Springs, CO 80905